Academic Legends in Biblical Theology,
Volume IV

The

I0078882

Daniel Hoax
Who Wrote Daniel?

J.C.W. West

Foreword by J. I. Packer

St. Catherine's Press ⊕ stcatherinespress.com

St. Catherine's Press

www.stcatherinespress.com

A set of books in preparation:

Academic Legends in Biblical Theology

Volume I: A Philosophical Overture: What is Truth?
Volume II: The Moses Enigma: What Are the *Toledot?*
Volume III: The Isaiah Conspiracy: Deutero and Trito?
Volume IV: The Daniel Hoax: Who Wrote Daniel?
Volume V: The Jesus Query: Language and *Logia*
Volume VI: The Gospel Puzzle: Who Wrote First?

Third edition

ISBN 978-0615657158

Copyright © 2016 by J. C. W. West

The cover picture is from
"The Handwriting on the Wall",
a painting by Rembrandt van Rijn (1606–1669)

To Rick, who first suggested this project
and has stuck by it through the agonies of
"Read a book and write a paragraph."
With love.

Table of Contents

Acknowledgments

I owe many debts of gratitude for helping me to bring this project thus far. Professor Allen Ross, now of Beeson Divinity School, was influential in the early trajectory of this study, as was the Right Reverend Alden Hathaway. I am also grateful for the insights of Old Testament professors Donald Collett and Erika Moore of the Trinity School for Ministry in Ambridge, Pennsylvania. Trinity's Dean/President Emeritus the Right Reverend John Rodgers, Jr., Th.D., gave me much encouragement, as did the Right Reverend C. FitzSimons Allison, D.Phil. (Oxon.).

I am not a biblical historian by training, nor has one reviewed the manuscript. Hence I invite feedback from readers on all aspects of the book—technical data and style. Roxanna C. West has been my advisor on matters Greek and Latin. Reading the manuscript as it progressed and giving valuable feedback were David Hull, M. B. Taintor, India Watkins, V. S. Geiger, B. P. Jeffries, B. P. West, and particularly my editor, Evelyn Bence. Finally, heartfelt gratitude to Al Cuneo, who is an absolute genius at designing covers for *Academic Legends in Biblical Theology* that will make the Legends set look as though a grown-up wrote the books.

I am grateful to them all.

J. C. W. West
Tallahassee, Florida
July 2016

Foreword

Satire is the literary equivalent of salt. Salt sharpens the taste of things but leaves a dryness in the mouth that many of us do not like, and sarcasm extended is similar. A little of it goes a long way; it generates a trade-off between short-term fun and long-term insight, which different people make differently; and thus, willy-nilly, the satirist gives hostages to fortune and risks seeming to trivialize matters of moment. There is a good deal of gentle satire in *The Daniel Hoax*, understandably so, since it answers self-inflating sceptics who think the book of *Daniel* really was a hoax from the start, and ought now to be exposed as such. But the core of West's book is serious historical argument, with theological implications, and it will be a pity if its stylistic fun keeps readers from appreciating its sober and constructive reasoning.

The author, a retired academic, argues against treating *Daniel* as a fictional second-century composition rather than a factual sixth-century record (BCE, of course), and shows tellingly how specific scepticisms have been whittled away by advancing scholarship, while warrants for receiving the book as Daniel's authentic memoirs, in the way Jewish and Christian exegetes have historically done, have piled up in strength. The competence of the presentation calls us to take it seriously.

In the task of upholding the historic Christian belief that the canonical Scriptures are what they claim to be—namely the true and trustworthy Word of God, our Creator's witness to his plans and ways in the form of variegated human witness to these realities—the book of *Daniel*, with its dramatic miracles and symbol-loaded predictions, has sometimes been felt as a weak and vulnerable link. That should not be, however, as the following pages show; information currently available points to a quite different estimate.

So is it reasonable in this twenty-first century to take *Daniel* at face value and believe what it tells us? Well, yes. Weigh West's scholarly discussion, and you will see.

J. I. Packer
Board of Governors Professor of Theology
Regent College, Vancouver, BC

Idiosyncrasies

Readership This project addresses several audiences. First are the interested laymen and students who are new to the *Daniel* dating and authorship issues and just enjoy a good mystery, complete with a bit of intrigue. I write with this first audience particularly in mind, trying not to leave them puzzling over terms that might be unfamiliar to anyone without biblical academic training. I trust that readers trained in academic theology will be gracious in patience, even when presented with more explanation than they need. Second are conservative academics and clergy and their followers who assume that *Daniel* was written when it implies it was. They are correct in their conclusion, but this little book may be able to add to their evidence for that conclusion. A third audience consists of modern academics and their followers who seem to ignore evidence unearthed during the twentieth century, or who seem oblivious as to how such evidence impacts the *Daniel* issues. I welcome them to the discussion and hope they will find it refreshing, though I am aware that sometimes one's investment in a Legend is too great to abandon. My expectations for this audience are modest.

Footnotes and Endnotes Footnotes at the bottom of the pages[1] are comments on the text. Endnotes with lower-case Roman numerals[i] are citations of the sources of information. As a reader, I hate to take time

---

[1] Like this. See how easy it is to read a footnote?!

to find a note at the back of a book, only to discover that it says nothing except the author, title, etc., or, worse, "ibid". On the other hand, I hate to read a book, ignoring the notes at the end because finding them interrupts my train of thought, only later to discover that some of them have interesting comments ...but not for me, because by then I have forgotten what the context was. I hope the reader does not find this arrangement distracting. The numbering of footnotes and endnotes is dictated by the software and is not specific to chapters.

Legends and Myths When capitalized, the word 'Legend' designates a doctrine or teaching *about* the Bible that is neither *in* the Bible nor implied by it, such as Q or *Deutero Isaiah*. I argue here that these Academic Legends are somewhat like Urban Legends: they are falsehoods that everybody believes because everybody else does. Here they are shown to be incorrect hypotheses that have been elevated into academic doctrines. A Maccabean-period *Daniel* is one such. Not capitalized, the words 'legend' and 'myth' refer to an ordinary myth or legend, such as a story about Greek and Roman gods; these words also appear when discussing whether some biblical characters might also be legendary, that is, not historical.

Scare quotes are double quotation marks used to emphasize a word or phrase and sometimes are used to substitute for the phrase 'so-called'. They are bad form according to a prejudice I inherited from a former professor[2] and are used here only in desperation or defiance.

Three sets of punctuation distinguish the titles of biblical books, their presumed authors, and the person for whom the book is called:

- The title in italics designates a **book title**; e.g., *Matthew* in italics is *The Gospel according to St. Matthew. Daniel* is the book of *Daniel,* etc.

- A term in plain roman letters refers to **the man** who was Daniel, a Jewish captive who became prime minister of Babylon and eyewitness to many events in three administrations (with no prejudice implied—or maybe just a little—as to whether the possibly legendary figure Daniel actually existed or actually authored *Daniel,* the book bearing his name).

- 'Daniel' in single quotation marks designates **the author(s)** of *Daniel* and necessarily did exist: (somebody[s] had to have written *Daniel*). It becomes obvious, therefore, that on many occasions Daniel and 'Daniel' are argued to be one and the same.

In direct quotations, these distinctions are not observed.

---

[2] Professor John Mulhern, formerly of the philosophy faculty of Bryn Mawr College.

Transliterations of proper names follow the usage of the author discussed or quoted--a result of cowardice.

Abbreviations

BC	Before Christ
AD	Anno Domine—the year of our Lord
BCE	Before the Common Era—BC
CE	Common Era—AD
OT	Old Testament
NT	New Testament
MT	Masoretic Text—the Hebrew language OT that is the standard text of the Jewish Bible
LXX	Septuagint—the second-century BCE Greek language translation of the Jewish Bible that predated the MT

1
Who Is Daniel?

"You don't seem to realize that ninety-seven percent of these authors disagree with you."

He was sweeping his arm at two of his office walls, shelves full of theological books. He was right in saying that they disagree with me. He was mistaken in assuming that I didn't realize it. "Your argument may have holes in it big enough for a Mack truck to drive through," referring to a book I was working on. Were there really holes in my argument? I was a retired teacher of logic at two universities, and had enough chutzpah to suspect that he had not bothered to read my manuscript, and that the holes he suspected in my argument were a mirage.

He was the academic dean of a seminary I was visiting for a semester precisely to investigate whether there were lapses in my arguments of which I was unaware. There might be some archaeological discoveries that would prove me wrong. If so, I wanted to be the first to know. Or there might be theological trains of thought that I should refute, but couldn't unless I knew about them. In this project I am working slightly outside the field in which I taught, which is philosophy. I specialized in roughly the same period as the Bible, but in Greece and Greek and classical logic, instead of Israel and Hebrew and biblical history.

The dean turned out to be gracious, personable, friendly, and helpful. In fact, he unknowingly alerted me to the fact that some biblical scholars, even in faculties of conservative seminaries, are among the dean's ninety-seven percent who are infected with Academic Legends about *Daniel*—and *Isaiah*, the Patriarchs, the Gospels, and Jesus' teachings. This may have been the most helpful thing he could do. These doctrines are each either true or false, and I want to find out which are which. A good library and scholars working in this area of study are nearly indispensable, particularly when these scholars disagree with my conclusions. Do they have information I am missing? Yes, but nothing damaging to any of my hypotheses so far.

Is the biblical book of *Daniel* a hoax? The dean's ninety-seven percent—victims and perpetrators of this Academic Legend—say it is. They were taught in graduate school that all the best scholars say that *Daniel* is a hoax. They all went off and wrote books on other topics, but taught their students that *Daniel* is a hoax because all the best scholars say that *Daniel* is a hoax. We get the picture.

Very few academicians have revisited the data recently. *Daniel*'s date is thought to be settled: S. R. Driver's *Daniel* (1900) seems still to be regarded as "the last word on *Daniel*".[ii] But Driver's book seems to be a linchpin for the dating of ancient Hebrew and Aramaic texts and also for analyzing the development of theological ideas. Since 1900 when Driver wrote, paleographers have transcribed clay tablets, Dead Sea Scrolls, and ancient papyri that in various ways give evidence that *Daniel* is not a hoax—evidence that *Daniel* was written in the sixth century BCE, not the second. So perhaps it might be time for the academic world to take another look. If *Daniel* is not a hoax, other Legendary assumptions need to be revisited.

Getting *Daniel* rightly adjusted into its proper historical niche will cause a small tremor in the biblical world. It will shift all the coordinates around just slightly, and the Global Positioning System of our biblical history will need to be readjusted. That is a terrible metaphor, because the planet doesn't have even a theoretical state of stability toward which its geology is adjusting, whereas history does. The past is past, and events occurred before and after other events. Getting them sorted out correctly is a worthy project with consequences. The discovery of the Judean desert scrolls (1940s) was a major historical tremor event, and more than fifty years later our scholarship is still readjusting to accommodate its findings. Whereas the scholarship before their discoveries was a sort of dogmatic wandering in a fog of partial information, assimilating them will help to verify *Daniel* either as a hoax or as a genuine historical document.

The basic story of Daniel is this: In the late seventh century BCE, a noble boy named Daniel was part of the royal household in Jerusalem, capital of Judah. In 605 BCE Nebuchadnezzar of Babylon won the Battle of Carchemish hundreds of miles away and acquired Judah among his spoils. He packed off to Babylon some treasures from the palace and Temple and some of the noblest people of the land, including Daniel. What with interpreting dreams and one thing and another, Daniel wound up as prime minister over all of Babylonia: that is, as ruler and chief prefect under King Nebuchadnezzar.[3] But as yet Daniel's name has not appeared in extrabiblical sources such as Babylonian clay tablets.

Several administrations after Nebuchadnezzar's death, his (probably) grandson-in-law Nabonidas became king and left his own son Belshazzar as viceroy while he, Nabonidas, spent several years in Tema at an Arabian Desert oasis in a remote corner of his kingdom, possibly nursing an embarrassing skin ailment.[4] On the very evening of a feast given by Belshazzar, the army of Cyrus, king of the Medo-Persians, liberated Babylonia, and Daniel again attained a position of influence in court.

In 538 BCE Cyrus issued a decree saying that Babylonia's captive peoples, including the Jews, were to go back to their respective native lands, reestablish their cities, rebuild their temples, and pay tribute (taxes) to Cyrus. As for *Daniel*, its author seems to be mentioned by name twice by Ezekiel, another captive in Babylonia. Other ancient Jewish literature also alludes to Daniel or *Daniel* several other times. Finally Flavius Josephus (37–100 CE), a Jewish writer in Rome, tells us Alexander

---

[3] The same king is spelled 'Nebuchadrezzar' in *Jeremiah* and *Ezekiel*, and 'Nebuchadnezzar' in *Daniel, 2 Kings, 1 Chronicles, Ezra, Nehemiah, Esther,* elsewhere in *Jeremiah,* and in *Ancient Near Eastern Texts,* ed. Pritchard. He conquered Egypt at the Battle of Carchemish, gaining all of Assyria's vassal states, including Judah.

[4] There is some speculation and very little evidence as to precisely why he was there and what his illness was.

the Great was delighted that when he visited the Temple in Jerusalem (332? BCE) the book of *Daniel* there predicted his victory over Xerxes.

So what is the problem? Well, the dean's ninety-seven percent have been spreading dastardly rumors about our friend 'Daniel': asserting that prophecies in *Daniel* must have been written in the second century BCE, after the events occurred because (they say) predictive prophecy is impossible. This notion is an Academic Legend. We now have evidence, my fellow sleuths, that 'Daniel' should not be charged with this hoax.

- o These critics are mistaken as to which events were being prophesied. Predictive prophecy is legitimate under a strict protocol which *Daniel* meets handily.
- o There were already copies of Daniel being circulated at the time when their assumed prophetic events occurred.

The rest of this little book is given to demonstrating that the dean's ninety-seven percent are mistaken about *Daniel*:

- o Some of the events predicted in *Daniel* are not the ones these scholars presume.
- o Their evidence against a sixth-century *Daniel* is mistaken..

Because they don't believe that God causes the future and upon occasion can have his prophets tell it out to all and sundry, these scholars must postulate that the book had to have been written after the events they assume it prophesied, but before there were any external evidences of the book. Until the Dead Sea documents were discovered in the 1940s there were no very old physical copies, so the date of its writing was somewhat nebulous. No longer.

Into the latter decades of the nineteenth century there was a widespread assumption that the Gospels were written by Apostles Matthew and John and second-generation disciples Mark and Luke. *Daniel* was mentioned in the Gospels and in the OT, so the issue of when *Daniel* was written was a non-issue: it was assumed that *Daniel* was written during the Babylonian exile, in the sixth century BCE. But the challenge of Higher Criticism (latter nineteenth century, at about the time of the American Civil War) theorized that the biblical texts were written at a time further and further removed from their traditional origins. Any text with Godly supernatural events became suspect. Scholars assumed that Gospel evidence and other first century mentions of *Daniel* would give a *terminus a quo*—the last date possible. But, the Higher Critics assumed, surely *Daniel* was a fabrication, by an author who couldn't even come up with original material. But . . .

2

Hoaxes and Sleuthing

… could there be hoaxes in the Bible?

Looking retrospectively at his own biblical education, in his book *Forged: Writing in the Name of God—Why the Bible's Authors Are Not Who We Think They Are* Bart D. Ehrman says, "When I was a conservative evangelical Christian at Moody Bible Institute in my late teen years, I knew for a fact that there could not be any forgeries in the New Testament."[iii] He goes on to tell his readers that three years later, at Princeton Theological Seminary, he came to think that he had been approaching the Bible the wrong way—that it should be approached as any other book, and examined for mistakes. He continues, by implication, to infer that anyone from Princeton can spot an error from a mile away.

> Human books from the ancient world sometimes contained forgeries, writings that claim to be authored by someone who did not write them ... The book of Daniel claims to be written, in part, by the prophet Daniel during the Babylonian captivity in the sixth century BCE. *But there is no way it was written then. Scholars for over a hundred years have shown clear and compelling reasons for thinking that it was written four hundred years later,* in the second century BCE, by someone falsely claiming to be Daniel.[iv]

Ehrman points out (correctly) that this view is almost universally held by critical scholars today. He recognizes that there are exceptions, citing Donald Guthrie, "who tries to argue on historical, rather than dogmatic, grounds" about alleged forgeries in the NT.[v]

It is on historical rather than dogmatic grounds that I argue here that Ehrman, along with the majority of biblical scholars today, is mistaken—even though he studied at Princeton—in claiming that *Daniel* is a second century BCE pseudepigraphon (hoax). The historical evidence shows that Daniel and *Daniel;* were on the scene long before the second century BCE. So to put down the Academic Legend going around that says *Daniel* was not written until the second century BCE as silliness, we look at data such as ...

- Josephus' contention that Alexander the Great saw a scroll of *Daniel* when he visited Jerusalem in about 331 BCE.
- *Ezekiel* mentions the man Daniel during the Babylonian exile (6th century BCE). Daniel cannot be the Ugaritic Danel we meet below.
- The evidence that the Jewish Great Assembly held that there was no prophecy in Israel from the time of *Daniel* in the Persian period.
- The Great Assembly probably canonizes *Daniel* and *Psalms* with the Prophets c 199 BCE. Later, the Great Assembly of 65 CE, shifted both to the (new) category of Writings.
- Several other biblical and extrabiblical ancient writers made allusions to *Daniel* or Daniel.

The Academic Legend is also mistaken as to what future events *Daniel* prophesies. Interpreters who are comfortable with predictive prophecy and its habitudes understand the fourth kingdom to be Rome, whereas those who restrict their interpretation to empires that appeared before the book did must somehow finagle the fourth kingdom to be Greece.

Daniel has two separate visions, one the dream of Nebuchadnezzar, and the other of Daniel the man, each with four successive symbols presumed to foretell great empires. In each case, Babylonia is the first. In chapter two, Nebuchadnezzar's wise men are all told not only to interpret the dream, but also to tell the dream itself. After all, anyone can invent a plausible interpretation; but one can know what someone else dreamed only if he is given superhuman insight:

> 2.[31]O king, as you looked on, there appeared
> a great statue. This statue, which was huge,
> and its brightness surpassing, stood before
> you, and its appearance was awesome. [32]The
> head of that statue was of fine gold; its breast
> and arms were of silver, its belly and thighs of
> bronze, [33]its legs of iron, and its feet part iron
> and part clay. [34]As you looked on, a stone was
> hewn out, not by hands, and struck the statue
> on its feet of iron and clay and crushed them.
> [35]All at once, the iron, clay, bronze, silver, and
> gold were crushed, and became like chaff on
> the threshing floors of summer; a wind carried
> them off until no trace of them was left. But
> the stone that struck the statue became a great
> mountain and filled the whole earth...

Ehrman and colleagues interpret the stone to be the Jewish Maccabean rebellion, and the pseudepigraphic Daniel to be a political broadside written at the time of

the uprising to enlist and encourage the Jewish populace to have heart and join the fight.

The book of Daniel tells us that the man Daniel, after
telling Nebuchadnezzar, successfully, the gist of his
dream, continued with its interpretation.

> [38b]You are the head of gold. [39]But another
> kingdom will arise after you, inferior to
> yours; then yet a third kingdom of bronze,
> which will rule over the whole earth. [40]But
> the fourth kingdom will be as strong as iron
> ...part potter's clay ...a divided kingdom ...
> [44]And in the time of those kings, the God of
> Heaven will establish a kingdom that ...
> shall last forever.[vi]

The dream of the statue with parts of precious and base
metals gives us one point of view of the kingdoms to
come. In chapter seven a second point of view is given
to 'Daniel' and its readers. Here the four[5] successive
kingdoms are depicted as different beasts. Chapter 7:

> 7.[2b]In my vision at night, I saw the four winds
> stirring up the great sea. [3]Four mighty beasts
> different from each other emerged from the
> sea. [4]The first was like a lion, but had eagles'
> wings. As I looked on, its wings were plucked
> off, and it was lifted off the ground and set
> on its feet like a man and given the mind of
> a man. [5]Then I saw a second, different beast,

---

[5] Four, or is it five? In verse 35 he speaks of "the iron, clay,
bronze, silver, and gold" as if each were a successive kingdom, yet the iron
and clay mixture seems elsewhere to depict a single empire. However, in
both passages he specifies four kingdoms, so we can safely assume only
four empires, with each having more than one successive ruler.

which was like a bear, but raised on one side, and with three fangs in its mouth among its teeth; it was told, "Arise, eat much meat!" 6After that ...there was another one, like a Leopard, and it had on its back four wings like those of a bird; the beast had four heads. and dominion was given to it. 7After that ... there was a fourth beast—fearsome, dreadful, and very powerful, with great iron teeth— that devoured and crushed, and stamped the remains with its feet...[I]t had ten horns. 8While I was gazing upon these horns, a new little horn sprouted up among them; three of the older horns were uprooted to make room for it. There were eyes on this horn like those of a man, and a mouth that spoke arrogantly. 9As I looked on,

> Thrones were set in place
> And the Ancient of Days
> > took his seat.
> His garment was like white snow
> And the hair of his head was like
> > lamb's wool.
> His throne was tongues of flame;
> Its wheels were blazing fire.
> 10A river of fire streamed forth
> > before Him;
> Thousands upon thousands
> > served Him;

The court ... sat, the books ... were opened. 11I looked on. Then, because of the arrogant words that the horn spoke, the beast was killed, its body destroyed and consigned to the flames. 12The dominion of the other beasts was taken away; but an extension of life was given to them for a time and a season...

> One like a human being
> Came with the clouds of heaven;
> He reached the Ancient of Days
> And was presented to Him.
> Dominion, glory, and kingship
>   were given to him;
> All peoples and nations of every
>   language must serve him.
> His dominion is everlasting, . . .
> And his kingdom shall not be
>   destroyed.[vii]

The statue's golden head, and the beast like a lion with eagles' wings, are classically deemed to refer to the Babylonian Empire (under Nebuchadnezzar and his successors). The statue's silver chest and arms, and the second beast (the bear with three fangs), traditionally are thought to represent the Medo-Persian Empire (under Cyrus the Great[6] and his successors). The statue's bronze belly and thighs, and the third beast— the winged and four-headed leopard—represent the Macedonian Greek Empire (under Alexander the Great and his four successors[7]). Finally, the statue's iron legs and feet with iron-clay amalgam, and the ten-horned beast with iron teeth with the arrogant small horn, was the Roman Empire (under the arrogant Augustus Caesar and his successors).

---

[6] Cyrus captured (1) his grandfather's Medo-Persia, (2) Croesus' Lydia, and (3) Nabonidus's/Belshazzar's Babylonia.

[7] There was some considerable jockeying at the start, but after the Battle of Ipsus (301 BCE) the fairly stable outcome of Alexander's military genius the Deodochi had four smaller empires: (1) Cassander, with Macedonia, Greece, Thrace, et al.; (2)Ptolemy, with Egypt and other nearby territories; (3) Lysimachus, with Lydia, Ionia, Phrygia, et al; and (4) Seleucus had Persia, Syria, et al.

'Daniel' lived to see only the first of these and part of the second. In *Daniel* chapter two this fourth empire—the Roman—is crushed and destroyed by a stone not made of human hands. St. Jerome (d 420 CE, scholar who translated the Bible into the Latin Vulgate edition) and others understand this stone to be the kingdom of God. Those who claim that *Daniel* was not written until after the predictions in it have come true—that is, in the second century BCE rather than the sixth century BCE—interpret the fourth empire to be the Greeks. It could not have been the Romans, according to their understanding that all prophecy had to be after-the-fact, because the book was already attested before Rome became an empire.

So they assume the fourth had to be the Greek regime of Antiochus IV Epiphanes. Antiochus IV Epiphanes in 168 BCE desecrated the Temple by making it a temple to Zeus and sacrificing swine on its altar, making it temporarily unfit for Jewish use. But is this what the Lord through His prophet 'Daniel' calls the "abomination of desolation"?[8]

There had been a worse such an abomination before Antiochus, and there would be a much worse abomination after Antiochus. In 587 BCE King Nebuchadnezzar insulted Judah by pulling down the walls of the city of Jerusalem, completely destroying Solomon's Temple, and carting the cream of the population off to Babylonia as slaves. The city of

---

8 Daniel 9.27, 11.31, 12.11; Ezra 9.1-4; Matthew 24.15-16.

Jerusalem and the Temple were rebuilt less than a century later under the grace and favor of Cyrus, the head of the Medo-Persian Empire. Antiochus, head of the Greek Empire (the bronze tummy and one of the four-headed panther's heads) desecrated the Temple with profane sacrifices, and it took eight days of miraculous multiplication of sanctified oil for the continuing Temple sacrifice, an event that would be memorialized as Hanukkah.

But the Roman general Titus and his forces—the iron-clay feet and bear with iron teeth—destroyed the Temple and carted the sacred vessels off to Rome.[9] They ransacked the city, and changed its name to Aelia Capitolina. Titus intended to desecrate the Temple by dedicating it to the worship of Caesar, but one of his soldiers accidentally set it on fire, destroying the Temple and ending the Temple sacrifice. Forever, presumably. Solomon's Temple was rebuilt some sixty years after its destruction (*Ezra* and *Nehemiah*), and its successor was rededicated only eight days after the insults of Antiochus (*I Maccabees* and *John* 10.22). But since the Romans under Titus destroyed it in 70 CE, it has never been rebuilt. Hence it is now 88,847.0625[10] times worse (and counting) than the Antiochus insult.

Those who interpret *Daniel* as late are hampered by their o'erweening assumption that the events it

---

[9] The Arch of Titus in Rome depicts a victory procession of the Temple gold.

[10] The number of years from August 70 to August 2016 (when I write this), times 365.25 days in a year, divided by 8 (the number of days it took to consecrate the oil for the rededication).

portends must have already happened before they were written. Hence the destruction of the Temple in 70 CE is not even in contention: everyone knows that *Daniel* was in circulation long before then.

The 97% also contend that the stone that destroyed this Greek empire was the Maccabean rebellion, led by the sons of John Hyrcanus, who fought against Antiochus and won. Antiochus was ousted in 165 BCE, and scholars who assume that *Daniel* was a hoax[11] say the book must have been written in about 164 BCE, describing these events. Some of the several fragments of Daniel text found among the scrolls at Qumran date from about 165 BCE. That in itself would be a full-fledged miracle if *Daniel* were a Maccabean period hoax.

Which event is the abomination of desolation, that of Greece (eight days) or of Rome (nearly two thousand years)? It seems obvious to anyone not blinded by an anti-prediction[12] prejudice that the far greater abomination is that of Rome. Is *Daniel* a hoax?

---

[11] I use 'hoax' because it is shorter than writing 'pseudepigraphon' (syood-uh-**pig**-ruh-fon—a fraud, a hoax. Literally, false writing). The reader should remember that the dean's ninety-seven percent of scholars argue that (1) writing pseudepigrapha (the plural form) was not uncommon in the 2nd century BCE, and that (2) *Daniel* was a pseudepigraphon. I agree with the former, that pseudepigraphia was not uncommon (nor reprehensible) at that time, but I demonstrate here that the latter is false. *Daniel* could not have been a hoax.

[12] Anti-miracle prejudice refuses to give God credit for weaving events together so that they work ultimate good for those who love God. (Ro. 8·28)

Hoaxes are fun for everybody except the ones who get snookered. And this role shifts from one level to the next. At the first level the hoaxer has fun pulling the wool over somebody's eyes. At level two are the ones who sniff out and expose a hoax for all the world to see. There is even more fun, with vindication piled on, for the one pulling the rug out from under the hoaxer.

But the most elegantly gleeful dance of all is a level three demonstration: Sometimes the ones who thought they were exposing a hoax were actually overzealous, and what they claimed to be a hoax was never false after all. Exposing the over-zealous— showing that a maligned painting is genuine, or that the book of *Daniel* is what biblical tradition claims it to be—is fun indeed. Hoaxes of various sorts have exploded onto the scene: artistic, scientific, literary, and documentary.[viii]

Piltdown Man, for example, was a classic hoax[ix] that fooled nineteenth century anthropologists and the world. The *London Illustrated News* of December 28, 1912, was snookered when it announced this:

> A discovery of supreme importance to all who are interested in the history of the human race was announced at the Geological Society ... [T]he keeper of the Geological Department of the British Museum displayed to an eager audience a part of the jaw and a portion of the skull of the most ancient inhabitant of England ...the remains thus far recovered leave no possible doubt ...affording us a link with our remote ancestors, the apes.[x]

The *Illustrated News* was right about the importance of filling in our gaps in history, but wrong about the remains. They do leave doubt. To scramble the evidence, whether intentionally or out of oblivious dogmatism, is an insult to the progress of information about our past.

Sussex solicitor Charles Dawson, principal "discoverer" of Piltdown Man, was perpetrator of the Piltdown fraud—which actually consisted of pieces of a human skull and the jawbone of an ape, surrounded by stone tools. Harry Morris, an amateur archaeologist who suspected the hoax, provided the proof after his own death. Morris left a flint tool in his collection of paleolithic artifacts with a note, "Stained by C. Dawson with the intent to defraud (all)—H.M."[xi] And most were defrauded.

Before Piltdown Man was exposed as a hoax, several generations of students had learned that Piltdown Man was right in there with the Neanderthals in a line from the ancestors we share with the apes. In 1950 the Piltdown evidence was submitted to electron microscopy. By 1953 the hoax had been exposed. But for nearly fifty years the world collectively wallowed in a mire of misinformation about the history of mankind.

Exposure of such fakes became the default attitude of academics, not wanting to be fooled again. This may have contributed to the attitude of pervasive skepticism that has continued through the twentieth century and into the twenty-first. "Fool me once, shame on you. Fool me twice, shame on me."

The villain of *Provenance*, (a nonfiction book, but a page-turner) by Laney Salisbury and Aly Sujo, is a hoaxer who specialized in twentieth-century paintings. The provenance of a thing—a painting, a piece of cloth, a book—is the evidence for its history. Who owned it when? When did someone see it? What is its carbon fourteen date? What is its language pedigree?

A major part of this hoax involved corrupting the provenance of paintings by changing museum records. *Provenance* is a good read if you enjoy a story where the good guys win in the end, or if you like or dislike twentieth-century art, and particularly if you collect twentieth-century art. Ac-tually, if you are an art collector you may either wish you hadn't read it or be very glad you did. *Provenance* il-lustrates beautifully the evil of hoaxing beyond the mere economic and artistic damage done to those involved.

Skepticism is healthy. There is truth out there to be discovered, and getting at it is a good thing. Hoaxes deserve a comeuppance because they interfere with the evidence. Literary genres, handwriting, spelling, gram-mar and punctuation usages, not to mention evidence gained from wood grains, the chemical content of fin-ishes, the choice of materials, and the development of craftsmanship, can give us information about the march of civilization. A hoax—or a false charge of a hoax— often destroys or confuses the historical information needed to infer the development of art, literature, or ideas.

Any false assumption causes problems. For example, if *Daniel* were a hoax, paleographers and biblical historians would be wrong to see it as a datable example of sixth-century culture and language—both Hebrew and Aramaic. If it is not a hoax, if they place it in the second century, they make the opposite mistake.

None of the original autographs of the Bible are extant. All we have to go on are scribal copies. And it was an established practice for scribes to update text as they copied. Hence much of the paleographic evidence of the Bible is obscured by the ancient Jewish practice of scribal updating. For a collection of books possibly written over a period of a thousand years—possibly much longer—the OT is remarkably coherent. So it is no wonder that scholars not accounting for this practice should suspect fakes

For there to be fakes, there must have been genuine articles somewhere. For example, unlike nineteenth-century *literati*, most scholars nowadays are reasonably sure that William Shakespeare himself wrote most of the plays and poems that bear his name. Plato's work was also misattributed; nineteenth-century scholarship had most of his letters, for example, pegged as falsely Plato's. But twentieth-century scholars have now rehabilitated all but one, and have declared them genuine, the last time I checked. If *Daniel* is a fake, where is the genuine apocalyptic literature the author copied?

According to the late Thomas Hoving,[xii] the flamboyant art historian and head of New York's Metropolitan Museum of Art, it appears likely that there has been a steady growth in fakes and hoaxes from the time of the Egyptian pyramids (long before Nebuchadnezzar and Daniel) to the present day. Perhaps like a prophet, an artist is not without honor except in his own time, so that hoaxing may be a variant of dishonoring one's own. Rather than honoring artists who are creating our own artifacts, buyers often will pay more for what they think was made by someone already honored. "My recent acquisition is a hoax? Well, I paid good money for it, so don't tell anybody!"

Now a new work by Leonardo da Vinci (1452–1519) has been given to the world and demonstrated not to be fraudulent. As I write, it is not yet on permanent public display like Leonardo's *Mona Lisa* in the Louvre. But someday *La Bella Principessa* also will be present for the world to see. This portrait, which is not a painting but a drawing in several media, is of Bianca, illegitimate daughter of Duke of Milan Ludovico Sforza. She was bride of Galeazzo Sanseverino, Sforza's favorite general.

If the portrait's present owners had not been experienced collectors, had not enjoyed art experts as close friends, had not made the right connections, and had not had a few strokes of what seemed like extraordinary luck, the world might not have this Leonardo now. The portrait might have remained in obscurity and languished unrecognized for another five centuries—or forever.

Several art experts persistently proclaimed it to be a hoax, including those at Christie's auction house, along with Hoving and others at the Metropolitan Museum. It is human nature to defend one's own past judgments, much as a mother bear defends her cubs. So two teams of experts—at the museum and at Christie's—came to insist that the Leonardo claim was simply a money-grab on the part of the owners, Peter and Kathy Silverman, who are art collectors and dealers. For the Silvermans, proving that the *Principessa* is not a hoax was a three-year tour de force.

The Silvermans bought the piece for $19,000 from a dealer who attributed it to a nineteenth-century German school. As seasoned art collectors, the Silvermans immediately had it examined by a restorer who assured them that it was painted earlier—much earlier. From 2008 to 2011, with a little help from their friends and art contacts, the Silvermans discovered pieces of evidence that together make a watertight case for *La Bella Principessa*'s authenticity as a genuine work of Leonardo.

But all good plots must thicken. Where did it come from? The provenance—its history of ownership—goes back only to the mid-twentieth century. Its previous owner surmised that it had been a gift to her late husband from the art historian Bernard Berenson, her husband's friend and mentor. But she had no evidence—just an assumption. Her husband had never indicated any suspicion that it was a Leonardo, and both he and Berenson had already died before the suspicion arose.

To sell the piece the owner turned to Christie's, which had sold other paintings for her, and whose expertise she had every reason to trust. But Christie's representative dismissed it as a nineteenth-century piece, and she had no reason to think he was mistaken. For a piece of art that turned out to be worth millions, she received a relatively paltry sum at auction.

The gallery owner who bought it at auction had not simply accepted Christie's assessment, but had taken it to her contacts at the Metropolitan Museum, all of whom, including Hoving, assured her that it was indeed a nineteenth-century piece in the old style—legitimately painted to look like a Renaissance work. And yet it is not a nineteenth-century German Renaissance revival piece. It is a genuine Leonardo. Someday it may be permanently displayed in a prominent museum—perhaps the experts at the Metropolitan might acquire it (with dribbles of crow on their chins)—for all and sundry to see: a triumph of the genuine over the cry of "hoax!"

Why do people cry "hoax"? One reason is that we prefer to see ourselves as too sophisticated to be fooled, so we think, "Oh, it can't be a real Leonardo!" The main reason, though, is that the odds are much better for its being a fake than for its being a genuine Leonardo. For example, a Rotterdam museum acquired a painting as a Vermeer, for $4.7 million in 2012 dollars. It was a forgery by Han van Meegeren. Peter Silverman tells us that van Meegeren

> was about to be indicted by the Dutch government for collaborating with the Nazis during the war. The charge: he had sold Dutch patrimony—*Christ and His Disciples at Emmaus*, [alleged to be a] Vermeer —to the notorious Nazi art lover Hermann Goering. Revealing the secret of the forgery was the only way to exonerate himself! So, before the tribunal and to the incredulity of scholars and the world press, van Meegeren showed how he painted his "Vermeers," . . .[xiii]

Thomas Hoving allowed as how he almost believed that there were as many bogus art works as there were genuine ones.[xiv] That is probably hyperbole, but the general atmosphere feeds the tendency of many art critics to hold suspicion and cynicism as their default attitudes. This perspective has bled over into other fields of scholarship, notably here what theologians call 'Higher Criticism'—the study of the sources, authorship, and background of the books of the Bible.

Suspicion about biblical provenance is not new. The neo-Platonist philosopher Porphyry of Tyre, in the third century CE, suspected that anything biblical that was thought to have originated before the Babylonian exile—the Pentateuch, the Prophets, and most of the Writings—was fraudulent, because everything before that era had to have been lost in the move to Babylonia. This itself would of course not have affected *Daniel*, but, as we shall see, Porphyry found other reasons to suspect *Daniel*. Caught up in the hoax epidemic, the twentieth-century Scandinavian School, led by Thomas Thompson, dates the original composition of everything in the Bible to the fifth century BCE or later. The thundering herd is never far behind them.

Recently two apropos hoaxes have come to my attention, both headlined in the *Wall Street Journal*. First, "How the 'Jesus' Wife' Hoax Fell Apart" references a supposed scandal in Christianity announced by Harvard Divinity School professor Karen King. The *Harvard Theological Review* published a group of papers attesting to the papyrus's authenticity. But experts in Coptic manuscripts found issues:

    First, the fragment shared the same line

> breaks as the 1924 publication. Second,
> the fragment contained a peculiar dialect
> of Coptic called Lycopolitan, which fell
> out of use during or before the sixth century
> ...The fragment was written in a dialect that
> didn't exist when the papyrus it appears on
> [7th to 9th c] was made.[xv]

According to the article, the consensus is that Professor King and the Harvard Divinity School were victims of the hoax, not its perpetrators.

The other recent headline is, "A Rembrandt Becomes a Rembrandt Again". Rembrandt's portrait of Dirck van Os (c. 1658) has been re-canonized.

> ... [A]rt historians of the postwar period
> leaned toward deattributing questionable
> Old Master paintings—a trend that reached
> its apex in the 1970s—with the result that
> many dubious pictures were usefully pruned
> ...Unfortunately, good pictures ...were
> sometimes tossed out of the canon, too.[xvi]

Daniel and the Rembrandt had something in common: both became encumbered with unoriginal material. In the case of the Rembrandt,

> Earlier generations of restorers embellished
> the sitter's sober attire by adding decorative
> lace to his simple linen cuffs and collar, a gold
> chain and cross to the front of his coat, a tas-
> sel to his staff, and a bit of white shirting in
> place of his vest. All of these elements were
> poorly painted ...leaving the painting as a
> whole looking muddled.[xvii]

Daniel, too, had gratuitous additions, particularly in its LXX (and other early Greek) translations.

> The medium-sized expansions of Daniel

were ...left in the text (4:17a, 33a-b, 37a-c).
However, two book-sized appendices were
placed at the beginning or end of the book
(Susanna, Bel and the Serpent). While the
large Expansion named "The Prayer of Azariah
and the Song of the Three Young Men" was
left in the text between 3:23 and 3:24 but given
deutero-canonical status.[xviii]

Although its Greek translations contain accretions added by
Greek language scribes or translators, the Masoretic Text
that we have today may be very close to the autograph, or at
least the official Temple edition, of *Daniel* that the priests
showed to Alexander the Great in about 332 BCE. This
investigation is different from Piltdown Man, *La Bella
Principessa*, or a fraudulent stock market transaction.

There is no *Daniel* autograph manuscript available for
carbon dating. Candidates for each kind of fraud require several areas of expertise to tease out the truth.
In the case of *Daniel*, expertise in the history of Hebrew
and Aramaic languages is applicable, and we see below
that not only can scholars take issue with one another's
application of such analyses, but that the historic
language evidence changes as more data come to light.
S.R. Driver can argue (below) that *Daniel*'s Aramaic is
anachronistic for the sixth century, whereas Driver had
no way of knowing, when he wrote in 1900, that nearly
fifty years later the Genesis Apocryphon would appear
among the Qumran texts and prove him mistaken.

But in each case, the truth is there somewhere. Either
the Hebrew–Aramaic Text of the book of *Daniel* found
at Qumran was written fraudulently (i.e., pseudepi-
graphically) in the second century BCE, or not.

So we continue our pursuit of hoaxes, frauds, false frauds, and false hoaxes. I think the reader will come to recognize that *Daniel* is a false hoax.

3

Porphyry of Tyre

The ancient city of Tyre has minor but recurring roles in our overall discussion of the person and work of Daniel. Tyre is now modern-day Sur, a city on the coast of Lebanon with five-star hotels, a beautiful sunset, and probably more than a *soupçon* of political unrest. Until Alexander the Great connected island to shore with a causeway, Tyre was a prominent island seaport off the coast of Lebanon.

- o In this chapter it plays its most recent role, as the home of Porphyry of Tyre, the third-century philosopher and avowed detractor of Judaism and Christianity.

- o Half a millennium earlier, 332 BCE, Alexander the Great besieged and conquered Tyre in his campaign down the Mediterranean coast. Its inhabitants initially accepted him without a fight but denied him access to the Tyrian temple dedicated to Ammon, whom he alleged to be his ancestor. This brought out his ire, particularly over his obsession with temples and their cultus. Alexander may have made a visit to Jerusalem during his siege of Tyre. Or not.

- o Earlier yet, during the sixth-century BCE Babylonian period, 'Ezekiel' admonished the proud prince of Tyre, comparing him to Daniel.

- o Nearly seven centuries before that, in the thirteenth century BCE, we encounter Tyre as the prominent city of the Phoenicians, the sea-going merchants who probably did *not*

> perpetuate *The Tale of Aqhat* and Aqhat's father,
> Danel of Ugarit, which was a neighboring port
> of Tyre (and of whom, more later).

That these all included Tyre is mere coincidence. None of these events had anything to do with any of the others. They could have happened in four different cities and not tried to confuse us. But they didn't. The reader is forewarned.

The most recent of these, Porphyry of Tyre, has become something of a hero to some modern biblical scholars. He is credited as being the first scholar to question *Daniel's* authenticity. Consequently, I use his name as shorthand to indicate those who think that *Daniel* is a hoax. Here they are porphyrists. This label does not imply that they follow Porphyry's lead on anything other than the dating of *Daniel*.

Until 1947 the physical provenance of *Daniel* manuscript copies went back only to the eleventh-century CE Leningrad Codex. Then archaeologists acquired copies that date from the three centuries before the destruction of the Jerusalem Temple in 70 CE. In the late 1940s and since, archaeologists have acquired several copies and fragments of *Daniel* from Qumran and other Judean desert sites, known popularly as the Dead Sea Scrolls—along with copies of other Scriptures, legal documents, personal letters, and grocery lists that date from the first and second centuries BCE and the first century of the Common Era.

In Jerusalem and elsewhere among Christians and Jews until the seventeenth century, nearly everyone seems to have assumed that the book of *Daniel* was written by its protagonist, Daniel, who lived in Babylon during the captivity of the Jewish people in the sixth century BCE.

In the third century CE the anti-Jewish and anti-Christian philosopher Porphyry of Tyre read *Daniel* in one of its Greek translations (probably the LXX [Septuagint] translation) and decided that the uncanny prophecies found in parts of *Daniel* were too accurate to have been written before the events he assumes they describe. Therefore they must have been written after those events occurred. In the Greek translation of *Daniel* that Porphyry read, some of the predictions may indeed have been written after the fact. E. B. Pusey (more of him later also) points out that some of the second-century BCE translators of the Greek OT manifestly glossed (added to) the biblical texts, including that of *Daniel*,[xix] inserting bits and pieces of what was, by the translator's time, history, so that his readers could understand it better. The Jewish translator(s) in Hellenistic Alexandria, Egypt,[13] inserted clarifications to make the narrative easier to understand, or to amplify its effect, by making the prophecies seem uncannily accurate. The LXX translators also omitted or changed statements they thought would be unacceptable to readers, and modified some doctrines.

Pusey observes that the LXX translator made both

---

[13] The reader will appreciate the problem here. Despite the tradition that has seventy-two scribes translating the LXX independently of one another and providing identical translations, there are several Greek translations of the Hebrew Bible, with various textual differences. I confess to the reader that I don't have access to the documents to know whether they all agree on the points at issue here or not.

Nebuchadnezzar and Darius, for example, appear more religious and more thoroughly converted to the worship of the Jewish God than does *Daniel*. The LXX also construed the insanity of Nebuchadnezzar as punishment for his sacrilege against the house of God—a gratuitous commentary influenced by his own political milieu.

This was an unintentional hoax-like deception, not intended to deceive but to enlighten. Instead, like all hoaxes, it scrambled the evidence. For example, the translation of the historical prophecy in *Daniel* 11 portrays one part too well—that which a Jew, living in Alexandria, Egypt, would have known. It expands the Hebrew narrative "there shall come ships of Kittim"[14] as "And the Romans shall come and shall expel him, and shall rebuke him strongly," accurately describing the way Popilius cut short the subterfuges of Antiochus Epiphanes.[15] This not only unintentionally pointed toward *Daniel* as being a bit too precise at this point, but also seems to pinpoint the fourth empire as Greek. After all, it was glossed during the Greek period, and the over-eager Greek translator thought that his own tyrant seemed very much like *Daniel*'s prophecy. (It always looks like the end of the world to those living at any time: there are always famines, earthquakes and wars and rumors of war.) But like the Three Billy-goats

---

[14] Scholars debate as to where this Chittim/Kittim is, although most assume it alludes to Rome, a piece of circular reasoning in this context.
[15] In 168 BCE the Seleucid king Antiochus IV prepared to attack and capture Alexandria, which angered the Roman Senate. They sent Popilius Laenus to bring him to heel. Popilius drew a circle around Antiochus in the sand, telling him not to broach it without giving him an answer to take to the Senate. Antiochus decided to withdraw from Egypt. Livy, Book 29, 45, 12.

Gruff, an abomination was coming after this one that was much bigger and more desolate indeed.

It is no wonder that Porphyry, reading the book in its scribally edited Greek translation(s) thought that the prophecies were written about Antiochus IV, and after the fact. Some of them were. But not by 'Daniel'; rather, the LXX was over-enthusiastically mistranslated here, and it may have been at least partially this that misled Porphyry—this and his own anti-Jewish zeal. Pusey says that a literal translation would, of course, have "guided him aright" on these points, although it would not have ridded the book of predictive prophecy, of which *Daniel* has much. But Pusey suggests that on whatever ground, down to the time of Antiochus Epiphanes, the LXX translator almost always distorts the facts, because he would not trust himself with a literal translation.[xx] So though Porphyry was apparently the first to cry "hoax!" about *Daniel*, he has some justification. Porphyry must have had followers in his own day, but I know of no Jewish or Christian writers who were con-temporaries of Porphyry who agreed with him about the dating of *Daniel*. In fact the Christians went so far as to burn his books on this subject. We know of them only from passages that his contemporaries (Jerome et al.) quoted in order to refute them.

One might ask, Isn't it a little tricky to know what Porphyry really said, if his works survive only through his dissidents? Yes, but there is now good reason to think that his detractors quoted him accurately. 20th century paleography such as the Nag Hammadi and Oxyrhynchus is finding copies of the targets of early Christian diatribes against heresy were quoted, cited, and interpreted quite accurately. Yet here it doesn't matter what he "really said". It is porphyrism[16] itself that is at issue, both then and now. But weep thee not, Fair Maid, for Porphyry: he was not of thine ilk. He believed in elves and spirits and practiced witchcraft, not modernism. He wouldst not have been thy friend. M. V. Anastos notes that Porphyry should have no affinity with Christians or modernists.

> [T]here are no grounds for assuming, as some have done, that Porphyry was well-disposed toward Christ but hostile to his disciples and the Evangelists, who were not the historians, but rather the inventors, of the episodes they set forth from the life of Jesus.[xxi]

Porphyry rejected the Evangelists and also rejected Jesus as an invention of the Christians. And he didn't stop there. He also rejected all of the Old Testament books written before the Babylonian captivity. Arguing that anything before that event would have been lost or burned in the destruction of Jerusalem, he claimed that the books of Moses and the Prophets as they stand to-day were written after the return to Judah in the fourth through the second centuries. Porphyry assumed, incor-rectly, that the Temple Scrolls would not have been brought to Babylon either on the orders of Nebuchad-nezzar (along with the Temple vessels) or by the Temple priests. He seems to have been misled by what I think of as a 'backpacker's syndrome': the notion that

---

[16] The terms 'porphyrism' and 'porphyrist' are not used pejoratively, in and of themselves. Only Porphyry's *Against the Christians* was destroyed on purpose. Many of his other works remained, and his book on Aristotelian logic was the standard textbook on the subject for centuries. B. S. Childs notes, below, that porphyrism has theological implications, which are discussed here in some depth in the penultimate chapter.

'biblical' means 'primitive' and that 'primitive' means 'stripped to the basics'—to the extent that they all traveled with the handles of their toothbrushes cut short, the better to fit them into sandwich-sized plastic zip bags for their backpacks.

Apparently this version of primitive was not the case. Daniel had a copy of *Jeremiah* in his library (9:2)[17] and may have had copies of all the to-be-Scriptures then written. His library copies may have been made in Babylon, but texts had to have been brought to Babylon either by Babylonian officials or by the Temple priests (or both). It is possible that their journey from Jerusalem to Babylon was by camel caravan and was fulsome with impedimenta of all sorts—including not only the Temple sacred vessels but also its library of scrolls. Nebuchadnezzar probably would have wanted the best of the Jewish scholars, along with the tools of their trade—their sacred writings.

So there we have it with Porphyry. The overzealous mistranslation into the Greek of the LXX gives the original impetus for characterizing *Daniel* as prophecy *ex eventu*. The prominence of academic disbelief in a sovereign God promotes it to a dogma and a faith. Nevertheless, fifteen to nineteen centuries later, Porphyry's dating of *Daniel* has won many followers among academic biblical scholars. In this, Porphyry probably gets more credit than he deserves. Porphyrism—the notion that *Daniel* must have been written during the reign of Antiochus IV Epiphanes—

---

[17] Of course this assumes that 'Daniel' is believable.

would have held sway over modern biblical theology without Porphyry. All it requires is either a belief in a god who created the world and then left it to its own devices, or a conviction that there is no such being as a God who is sovereign over time and space. (For more on this issue, see Chapter 13.) The age of modernism, beginning roughly with Des-cartes (1596–1650), decreed that neither man nor God can know the future: predictive prophecy is impossible. Hence any predictive writing must be either intention-ally fiction, such as science fiction, or intentionally some other kind of fantasy such as the novels of C.S. Lewis or George MacDonald. But predictions that seem to come true must be forgeries written after the events they purport to portray.

What events do his critics think 'Daniel' is trying to portray? Many scholars from the seventeenth through the twentieth centuries agree that *Daniel* must have been written during the Maccabean rebellion, just after Anti-ochus IV Epiphanes (reigned 175–164) desecrated the Temple by dedicating it to the worship of Zeus and by sacrificing swine on its altar—an act the scholars have thought must be the referent of *Daniel*'s term tradition-ally translated 'abomination of desolation'.[18] Porphyry thought *Daniel* was written in about 165 BCE. But is Antiochus' abominable action the 'abomination of desolation' that *Daniel* prophesies? Perhaps.

But it probably is not. Much more abominable and

---

[18] Dan. 9:27 "He shall cause the sacrifice and the oblation to cease ...to the full end, shall wrath be poured out upon the desolate"; see also 11:31; 12:11.

thousands of times more desolate is the destruction of the Temple by the Roman army in 70 CE under Titus. Antiochus desecrated it, yes, but only for it to be cleansed and rededicated, and the sacrificial system established again in a mere eight days. Antiochus' desecration was a mere blip—a much lesser event than even the destruction of Jerusalem and leveling of the Temple under Nebuchadnezzar in 586 BCE. At the direction of Cyrus the Great the second Temple was rebuilt in 516 BCE, though not with its former Solomonic grandeur. Its architecture was enhanced under Herod the Great in the first century BCE.

Why do the porphyrists award Antiochus the prize? Because the destruction of Nebuchadnezzar truly was history for 'Daniel', and there is voluminous evidence that by the time of Titus *Daniel* was already written. It was referred to in the New Testament, written before 70 CE, and multiple copies of the book were found among the Dead Sea Scrolls, archaeological sites that predate Titus. So for *Daniel* to refer to Titus' destruction of the Temple would have been predictive prophecy, whether written in the 6th or the 2nd century, and porphyrists cannot allow predictive prophecy.

That is only one example of the wobbly interpretation of the *Daniel* prophecies required by porphyrism. Jerome demonstrates in his commentary on *Daniel* the multiplicity of interpretations of *Daniel*'s prophecies. Jerome says of Nebuchadnezzar's dream image (Dan. 2), representing rulers and empires:

o   The head of gold is identified in the text (v 38) as Nebuchadnezzar's kingdom.
o   The empire made of silver is that of the

- Medes and the Persians.
  - The third, of bronze, is the Alexandrian empire, that of the Macedonians, and of Alexander's successors ... It signifies not only the fame and power of the empire but also the eloquence of the Greek language.
  - Now the fourth empire, which clearly refers to the Romans, is the iron empire which breaks in pieces and overcomes all others ... iron and earthenware ... most clearly demonstrate at the present time.[xxii]

Isaac Newton (1642-1727) is as confidant about their identity as is Jerome:

> ... this vision of the image composed of four Metals, ... represents a body of four great nations, which should reign over the earth successively, viz., the people of Babylonia, the Persians, the Greeks, and the Romans.[xxiii]

Everyone acknowledges, including Porphyry and modern porphyrists, that *Daniel* was already written before the advent of the Roman Empire on the 5th of February in 2 BCE, ushered in by Pontifex Maximus and Pater Patriae Caesar Augustus (63 BCE-AD 14). Therefore Porphyry and the modern porphyrists say that this fourth empire must be the Greeks, because 'Daniel' could not have predicted the Roman Empire. Greece is the empire under which the Maccabees revolted and under which the hoaxist author, pseudo-'Daniel', must have written.

The reader will notice that this is circular reasoning. What is at issue here? Whether or not the Lord can empower 'Daniel' to predict the future. Why can the

Roman Empire not be the fourth empire? Because 'Daniel' cannot possibly predict the future. In logic, this is called *petitio principii*, or begging the question, or a circular argument. It is very common in ordinary thought. We get our minds so set on a certain point of view, such as the impossibility of predictive prophecy, that we don't notice when we use that notion as the very reason for its certainty. So it is with porphyristic reasoning: Greece must be the fourth empire, because 'Daniel' must write after the event has happened.

There are several ways the porphyrists have finagled to put Antiochus' Greeks as *Daniel*'s fourth empire in this passage. For example, "Let's give the Medes a separate empire from the Persians." This would not fit history, because the Median Empire as such was contemporary with the Babylonian. Or, "We could break the Greeks into two empires: Alexander's empire and the divided empire of his heirs." Again this is illegitimate. Each of the empires has several generations of rulers. But no matter.

Because porphyrists think that its author(s?) wove the book as a piecemeal fiction, they assume that 'Daniel' needed no authentic history to include in the four empires he credits in Nebuchadnez-zar's dream. After all, fiction is fiction, and a hoax is pure fiction. The only thing that porphyrism requires is four em-pires, however fictitious. He could have included Alice's Wonderland as an empire without porphyristic infidel-ity. Of course I jest. Critics assume that 'Daniel' is making an effort, however incompetent, to write an account that would seem at least plausible to his audi-ence of second-century BCE Jews. Finally, he has

○   A stone cut by no human hand smites the image, which disintegrates, whereupon the stone grows and fills the whole earth.

Over the centuries even this simple allegory in *Daniel 2:44–45* has not had straightforward interpretation. Jerome says,

> This last [the stone who crushes the iron empire] the Jews and the impious Porphyry apply to the people of Israel, who they insist will be the strongest power at the end of the ages, and will crush all realms and will rule forever.[xxiv]

So Jerome says that Porphyry in the third century CE and Jewish scholars, including those of his own time, held a consensus view that the stone (that was to smite the statue's feet) symbolized the people of Israel. But even so, this does not imply a consensus about what empire the stone would destroy.

What kingdom does Porphyry think the crushing stone will smite? It could not have been the Romans, or he would seem to have lost his objection to prediction. *Daniel* was written before the Roman Empire was born. Porphyry must have interpreted 'Daniel' to refer to the Jews' successful rebellion against the Seleucid Greek rulers (Porphyry's iron and clay empire), a rebellion that eventually issued in the Jewish rule of John Hyrcanus, high priest and ruler of Judea 135/134 to 104 BCE. This could have put Porphyry's date no earlier than 135, when there may have been (but Porphyry could not have known about) multiple copies of *Daniel* at Qumran.

It would not have bothered Porphyry to know, as he did, that the Hasmonean rule of Judea would neither fill the whole earth nor last forever. Porphyry assumed that 'Daniel' was a false prophet whose predictions failed. If 'Daniel' had been writing during the Maccabean period, he would not have known that the Jewish rebellion of that time would not be permanently successful. Meanwhile, Jewish scholars of the third and fourth centuries CE would have had no reason not to continue thinking that the Lord could raise up leaders like the Maccabees who would smash and overthrow the Roman Empire and issue in a future golden age of Jewish rule.

The Christian scholar Jerome, the fourth century Jews who were his contemporaries, Isaac Newton in the seventeenth century, and conservative scholars today, all interpret the iron and earthenware fourth empire to be the Roman Empire, which officially began before Jesus was born, and of which Judea under the Hasmoneans became a vassal state. This is not the reign of Antiochus IV of the Seleucid Greek Empire that the modern porphyrist takes to be the fourth empire, and that the Maccabean Jews revolted against. This is the Roman Empire that inspired later Jewish revolts, including the one that precipitated the siege and capture of Jerusalem under Titus in 70 CE. The Sicarii, under Eleazar ben Ya'ir, were defeated by Rome at Masada, 73 CE. Simon bar Kokhba led another Jewish revolt against Rome, and was defeated in 132 CE.

Jewish interpretation saw the crushing stone as the Mother of all Successful Jewish Uprisings. The Christians, including both 5th century Jerome and 18th century Isaac Newton identified it as the coming kingdom of

God against ungodliness. If it is either the Jewish or the Christian success over the pagan world, it seems to be already begun but not yet realized: it has been happening for two thousand years in what appears to be very slow motion. So there is no consensus as to the interpretation of *Daniel*'s prophecies.

But the plot thickens considerably in the twentieth century as to when the prophecies were made. In 1947 Hebrew University bought some scrolls from an Eastern Orthodox bishop who had bought them from an antiquities dealer who had bought them from some Bedouin who said that shepherds found the ancient scrolls in caves overlooking the Dead Sea. Scholars determined that they were dated between the second century BCE and the Romans' assault on Jerusalem in 68 CE. These Dead Sea caves became archaeological sites, where numerous texts of *Daniel* were found that pushed the *Daniel* provenance back to about 170 BCE and upgraded it from references in other texts to physical copies of the *Daniel* text (but not of course the autograph). That is squeaking the Dead Sea copies very close to—if not before—the date when porphyrists say that the original *Daniel* must have been written. The Dead Sea *Daniel*s should do away with porphyrism.

But they seem not to have done so. Most theology professors at mainline seminaries still assume that *Daniel* is a fraud. The question here addressed is whether 'Daniel' was a circa 165 BCE author, writing political commentary disguised as boiler-plate apocalyptic texts along with everyone else, or was he a sixth-century genius, writing the earliest fully developed apocalyptic texts, as a God-inspired high governmental official, writing his firsthand account of God's action in international history. Which author pioneered the apocalyptic genre? Some-body had to have been the first. Might it not be 'Daniel'? And might he not have been writing his own story? Winston Churchill did. Churchill had contemporary corroboration of his prescience. So did Daniel (infra, chapter 13), but his detractors, centuries later, don't accept the contemporary corroborations of Daniel's career as an administrator. Perhaps clay tablets will someday emerge showing Daniel at Nebuchadnezzar's table or in Cyrus' entourage. Or not.

Porphyry's view now has been assimilated into that of modern critical scholarship.[xxv] John J. Collins, for example, writes that Porphyry's insight was resisted for more than a millennium, but its validity has been widely acknowledged by modern critics (including himself) from the eighteenth century to the present. According to Collins, Casey, Hartman, and others, *Daniel* refers to no events later than the time of Antiochus IV Epiphanes, who died in 164 BCE.[19] Porphyry himself set the date of *Daniel's* composition at 165 BCE, because he thought it included the recapture and rededication of the Temple, which occurred before the death of Antiochus; he includes Judas Maccabeus as the messianic figure and so considered these events to account for some of the text of *Daniel.*

---

[19] This date is precise because porphyrists identify Antiochus' dastardly deeds as the abomination described by 'Daniel'. But the circumstances of Antiochus' death are inaccurate of Antiochus, so they think 'Daniel' began predicting rather than recording at that point and got it wrong. That date puts the book's creation at the time when numerous copies had already been made and were found at Qumran. Ergo, porphyrism has a problem.

Daniel is not the only biblical book that surprised critical scholarship when multiple copies of it were found at Qumran. Multiple manuscripts of *Psalms* were also found there, including some psalms that had heretofore been judged as Maccabean—i.e., second century BCE —in date. Scholars have now abandoned the Maccabean dating of these "late" psalms and redated them to an earlier period, because these scholars assume that there is inadequate time for a Judean desert copy of a Maccabean-period composition. R. K. Harrison notes this double standard between the Qumran *Psalms* and *Daniel.*

> [E]ach song had to win its way in the esteem
> of the people ...Did *Daniel* not have to win
> its way in the esteem of the people also? [xxvi]

Porphyry has thus become something of a folk hero for the academic porphyrists—those whose natural inclination it is to see the Bible as entirely the work of uninspired men. Neo-porphyrism cannot be excused on the same grounds as Porphyry, though. Modern porphyrists have the Hebrew and Aramaic text of *Daniel* to study and cannot have been misled by an overly enthusiastic LXX translator's extrapolations and interpolations. Any second-century date poses problems that modern porphyrists seem to prefer to ignore. Porphyrism has now been seriously undermined by Near East archaeological studies and the Judean desert *Daniel* manuscripts.

4
Daniel in the Canon

Edward Bouverie Pusey was Daniel's advocate, Samuel Rolles Driver his accuser and prosecutor. Hence Driver has become the patron saint of modern porphyrism, and Pusey their whipping boy. Both men wrote before the development of 20th century archaeology. In the next two chapters we will see that Driver's case against a sixth century *Daniel* is mistaken in many of its points, and that much of Pusey's case for a sixth century *Daniel* has been supported by subsequent archaeological findings. The chief reason for this seems to be Driver's preference to ignore evidence from early witnesses on the grounds of their ignorance. Recent vindication of the accuracy of these early witnesses, and Pusey's acceptance of their evidence, has stood him in good stead.

Pusey (1800–1882) was Regius Professor at Oxford, a Tractarian, a canon of Christ Church College, and the theologian for whom Pusey House at Oxford was named. He wrote a comprehensive critique on *Daniel*, arguing cogently against Porphyry and marshaling the information available in 1868. To his disadvantage, Pusey writes in a turgid, opaque style, with no obvious effort to show his reader the skeleton of his argument. Nor does his book have an index. So even those who want to apprehend Pusey's wisdom on *Daniel* must follow him with determination. He makes the case that

Daniel is correctly ranked among the Writings in the Jewish Bible, the Tanakh, [20] because it has the properties of the other books in that category.

Some thirty-two years after Pusey wrote his book on *Daniel,* Driver (1846–1914) led the vanguard of modern porphyrism with his own commentary on *Daniel,* written for school students, which is a scathing Broad Church critique of Pusey [xxvii] about which Childs says,

> It was S.R. Driver's commentary of 1900 which broke the back of the conservative opposition. In his lucid style and meticulous scholarship Driver mounted the case for Maccabean authorship. [xxviii]

Driver's style is lucid, skeletal, and replete with italicized emphases. He assumes that *Daniel* is in style a prophetic work, despite the fact that (as Childs and others assume its prophecy is spurious. Daniel is called a prophet in ancient Jewish texts found at Qumran and in the NT, written at about the same time. He writes prophecies. So he must have been a prophet.

The Tanach, which is essentially the Christian Old Testament, is organized differently from the OT. It is divided into the Torah, the Prophets, and the Writings, and the Tanach classifies *Daniel* among the Writings, not the Prophets. Driver contends that if *Daniel* had already been written when the Prophets were canonized, it would have been included among the Prophets. It is not included in the Prophets, therefore it must not have

---

[20] Just as 'Nabisco' is short of National Biscuit Company, 'Tanakh' is short for the Hebrew *Torah* (Law), *Nevi'im* (Prophets), and *Ketuvim* (Writings).

been written at the time. What Driver did not know was that the Prophets were made holy—canonized—before the Writings, and that both *Daniel* and *Psalms* were indeed included in the Prophets until the Writings category was instituted, probably not until 65 CE.

Pusey's contention is that the books contained in the Prophets division were written by men to whom it was their God-given full-time job to prophesy. The biblical category labeled Prophets contained works by men whom God called to a lifelong career as His spokesmen on various topics. The category that was labeled Writings, on the other hand, were works by or about Jewish people of high rank, whether some of their writing was prophetic or not. Daniel's career—his day job—was administrative, as Prime Minister of Babylon under Nebuchadnezzar. Under Darius[21] and Cyrus he was possibly an official advisor of some sort. His prophesying was part-time—something he did only when the Lord gave him a prophetic task.

Driver's contention is that the rabbis who made the decisions about the arrangement of biblical books were mistaken—that he himself has a better understanding of the rationale for categorization of the biblical books than did the first century rabbis. They unknowingly miscategorized *Daniel* because it was written after its proper category—Prophets—was finalized. Who was right, Pusey or Driver?

---

[21] More about this name below, as to whether this "Darius" was a viceroy of Cyrus or it was another name for Cyrus himself. Should 'and' here be in fact 'that is,'?

About this, they were both right about some aspects,
and they were both confused, as we see in the light of
the Qumran discoveries and elsewhere. Both *Daniel* and
Psalms apparently were at first canonized (i.e., declared
holy) among the Prophets, and then later they were
both promoted to the Writings, possibly based on the
qualifications of nobility that Pusey suggests (perhaps
subconsciously on the part of the rabbis). Or the
classification could have been based on some obscure-
to-us liturgical criterion having to do with Temple
protocol that is, or is not, in the early rabbinical
literature. We should never underestimate our ignorance and blindness about historic data.

Psalms seems to have made a similar canonical journey:
included with the Prophets until the Writings were instituted. Are the psalms authored by the nobility? Yes,
many are attributed to David, and as a book, they are all
Davidic as a genre. Might psalms be prophetic? Yes, all
tell forth God's message to mankind. Some are praise,
some lamentations, some contain predictive prophecy.
There is probably nothing in the Bible more authentically predictive than Psalm 22, predicting Jesus' crucifixion:

> [15] ("I thirst") My tongue sticks to my cheek,
> you have brought me to the dust of death.
> [16] They pierced my hands and feet. [18] They
> divided my garments among them, they drew
> lots for my clothes.

No one can make this up. It is not *vaticinium ex eventu*:
the psalms were already at Qumran in black and white
on papyrus or parchment before Jesus was crucified.
Nor did Jesus read this psalm and then organize the
piercing of his hands and feet, or the gambling for his

clothes, to tick off the psalmist's account of his crucifixion. The author of the psalm, was prophesying that
event possibly a thousand years before it happened, before the practice of crucifixion came into use. Even if
this particular psalm is not of David's authorship, nevertheless it was in a bookroll at Qumran when an obscure Galilean was crucified, fulfilling its prophetic
phrases.

Pusey observes that the Writings are a collection of the
works by and about kings and high officials:[22]

Psalms	King David (et al.)
Proverbs	King Solomon (et al.)
Song of Songs	King Solomon (et al.)
Ecclesiastes	King Solomon (et al.)
Daniel	Prime Minister of Babylon
Ezra-Nehemiah	Prime Minister of Judea
Ruth	David's great-grandmother
Chronicles	Royal decrees?
Lamentations	Jeremiah? If so, why?
Job	Nobility?

The final three of this list are puzzling to me. Did the
rabbis who categorized them know something about
them that I don't know? That may be the best answer. I
decline to assume that I know more about the biblical
background than did those who made these decisions

---

[22] One cannot help but wonder whether some of the Writings—notably *Song
of Songs, Proverbs, Ecclesiastes*, and some of the *Psalms*—would have become
canon (declared holy) had they not been attributed to David and Solomon.
They seem analogous to some recent paintings that are now canonical (i.e.,
collectible) because they were painted by Adolf Hitler; Winston Churchill,
Charles, Prince of Wales; and George Bush II, president of the US.

two thousand years ago. Pusey seems also to have declined that assumption, but not Driver.

Driver in effect deposed the rabbinical tradition, Josephus, the Catholic and Protestant divines, as well as Pusey's insights on *Daniel*.[23] Most porphyrists are quite comfortable with that result, and rely unquestioningly on Driver's conclusions. It is perhaps ironic that Driver, who was awarded the Pusey and Ellerton Scholarship as an Oxford undergraduate, and in 1883 succeeded Pusey as Regius Professor of Hebrew and canon of Christ Church, was to become Pusey's most prominent detractor.

Twentieth-century scholars have added nothing in the past century that might support Driver's argument except for proposing Danel-the-Rapha-Man as the "Danel" mentioned in *Ezekiel*. We see below that this is a non-starter. Archaeology, which was scarcely yet a new field of study when Driver wrote, has thrown porphyrism more gauntlets than bones. With little or no help from archaeology, and I suspect even less from paleography, biblical scholars nevertheless collectively assume that Driver's objections to a sixth-century *Daniel* are still valid.

But not all scholars agree. Several pieces of evidence that conflict with Driver's argument have been found in the twentieth century—most notably, the Dead Sea

---

[23] Driver published this in the *Cambridge Bible for Schools and Colleges*, so the succeeding generations of English clergy would have been taught Driver's interpretation of *Daniel* from their youth.

desert discoveries of biblical scrolls and other texts.[24] K. A. Kitchen (b. 1932), E. J. Young (1907–1968), Joyce Baldwin (d. 1996), Gleason Archer (1916–2004), D. J. Wiseman (1918–2010), and several other biblical scholars have subsequently shown that Driver is demonstrably mistaken about all but one point: namely, that nobody knows the identity of Darius the Mede. Yet.

Despite Wiseman's, Baldwin's, and Kitchen's measured and masterful refutations of Driver, as late as 1979 Brevard Childs (1923–2007) was still emphatic that Driver had said the final word on the historical issues surrounding *Daniel*—reminding us of the early-twentieth-century sage[25] who suggested that the US government could safely close the Patent Office, because everything that could be invented had already been invented. In what Childs calls "his lucid style and meticulous scholarship", Driver mounted the case for Maccabean authorship "in a way which appeared to most Englishmen not only to have successfully salvaged the book's religious value, but to have established definitively the critical position."[xxix] [26] And remember, "most Englishmen" cut their eyeteeth on Driver's commentary on *Daniel* with the *Cambridge Bible for Schools and Colleges*. Who would want to read Pusey, when Driver said his say with a fraction of the number of words?

---

[24] This assumes that Solomon Zeitlin is mistaken in ch. 14 below—a safe assumption, although on other topics Zeitlin gives useful information.
[25] He is Legendary, for all I know.
[26] I am puzzled as to how Childs thinks Driver has salvaged Daniel's religious value, when Childs himself observes, below, that Driver's argument has had quite the opposite effect on scholarship.

Driver begins his argument against the authenticity of
Daniel with the charge based on canonicity. This turns
out to be a more veiled and vexed topic than most
scholars expect.

> I – 1. The position of the book in the Jewish
> Canon, [is] not with the prophets, but in the
> miscellaneous collection of writings, called
> the *Kethubim*, or 'Hagiographa.' ...The collec
> tion of the 'Prophets' could hardly have been
> complete before the third century B.C.; and
> had the Book of Daniel existed at the time,
> and been believed to be the work of a proph-
> et, it is difficult not to think that it would
> have been ranked accordingly.[xxx]

It was indeed ranked accordingly. *Daniel* apparently was
listed among the prophets from 299 BCE when the
Prophets were canonized until after 65 CE, but Driver
did not count this information.

Many scholars think of the biblical canon as an arm-
chair exercise like theoretical mathematics that can be
resolved by lucid and persistent thinking about the
observable characteristics of the various books of the
Bible. But the rabbis and elders who made it happen
had other criteria. Driver assumes that if *Daniel* were a
sixth-century book, and if there are predictive prophecies in *Daniel*, the author should be considered a prophet and therefore the book should be categorized with
the Prophets. It is not now among the Prophets, therefore he concludes that it has never been so categorized,
and so had not been written at the time the Prophets
became canon, but later. End of story.

What is canon, anyway? The term 'canon' as used here may originally come from a Semitic word '*kaneh*', meaning 'reed' or 'stick', and then 'measuring stick', which evolved into a (Greek) '*kanon*' for measuring.

But the term 'canon' plays almost no part in the early rabbinical discussion, which instead focuses on *defiling the hands*. It roughly transposes into what academic biblical scholars call *canonicity*. The term 'canon' is complemented by the Latin '*classici*' which became a standard of quality, and the Greek word '*pinax*', at first a plank or slate, which became the list written on the slate. The catalogue of the library at Alexandria was the *pinakos*. These all came to refer to things that became the criterion of excellence for their class, whether poetry, rhetoric, sculpture, music, or carpentry. By implication, it is essential to the notion of canon or *pinakos* that some things were left out because they were found wanting. This also implies that there is a hypothetical standard by which examples are judged worthy or unworthy. The notion of standard is wrapped up in the notion of canon.

Perhaps the greatest biblical affinity is between the Protestant Christian Old Testament canon and the Jewish Tanach. But even here there are differences in categorization of the books. The scholars of the Reformation rightly took the Tanach as being more primitive—in the sense of older—than the Roman Catholic Bible. This included what we now know are accretions from the Septuagint, some of which are same accretions to which Porphyry objected, and it canonized these extra add-ons, declaring them to be Holy Writ.

The Protestant Reformers went to the Hebrew scriptures seeking authenticity of both text and content. The five books of the Law was kept as the Pentateuch in both Bibles, but when it came to the Prophets and the Writings, the Protestant Divines considered their own divinations to be more divine than those of the rabbis.

So instead of the Pentateuch, Prophets, and Writings (Torah, Nevi'im and Khetuvim = Tanakh) the Divines preferred the Law, the Historical books, and the Poetical books. While the Protestants sorted by the character of content, the Jews seem to have sorted by sources, as they came down via Tradition. Moreover, the criterion was, on its surface, ceremonial —how the reading of a particular scroll functioned in Temple cultus. Did it ceremonially defile the hands of the reader in the Temple liturgy or lectionary? By the intertestimental period, this question had become quasi-political and could be put to a vote of the Great Assembly.

We can now with some accuracy pinpoint the occasions when the various categories of biblical books were declared holy, that is, canonical. Some information here was not generally available at the time when Pusey and Driver wrote, because scholars erred in dating the rift between Judah and Samaria. This dating was adjusted by the Daliyeh papyri, discovered in a cave in 1962.

Many lay people, if they have been introduced to the history of canon at all, have been told that the OT canon was decided at the Council of Jamnia after the Fall of Jerusalem to Rome in 70 CE. Not so. The Jamnia (Yavneh) event is almost certainly a figment of recent scholarly imagination. The group of rabbis in Yavneh (a small town west of Jerusalem) after Jerusalem fell may probably have been more like a neighborhood coffee house where rabbis met to discuss things— probably *con brio*, but with no official authority.

The formal processes happened a few years before the fall of Jerusalem, while the Temple was still functioning, and are rooted in passages such as that beginning at Numbers 19:11 concerning the issue of ritual cleanliness. It says there that touching a dead human body causes a man to become ritually unclean, or defiled, for seven days, so that he must leave the camp, and cleanse himself with water on the third and seventh days. It then tells how he can again become clean, so as not to defile the tabernacle.

For the Jews, the Torah was considered sacred from the time Moses placed the books (stone slabs? clay tablets?) in the Ark of the Covenant. But defiling the hands seems not yet to have been part of the definition of sacred. The practice of a ritual, liturgical reading of the books aloud to the assembled people seems to have been sporadic at first and not a regular part of the wilderness tabernacle cultus, which originally seems to have been primarily sacrificial. From the beginning, though, when Moses read the Torah it seems to have been within a sacred setting, after burnt offerings and peace offerings (Exod. 24):

> 23 Moses took half of the blood and put it in basins, and half he sprinkled on the altar, 24 and he took the book of the covenant and read in the hearing of the people; and they said, "All that the LORD has spoken we will do."

It was nearly a thousand years later, after the return from Babylonia, that the Pentateuch was officially declared holy. [27] According to Solomon Zeitlin (1886–1976), and there seems to be general agreement on this:[28] the Pentateuch was canonized at the time of Ezra.[xxxi] Seventy of the elders of Israel are mentioned (Neh. 9:38). They "make a sure covenant and write it", and the nobles, Levites and priests seal it. This is the Great Assembly, which met at the time of Ezra, 444 BCE (Neh. 10:1–27), nearly a century after the Second Temple foundations were laid. These joined with the people and covenanted to be loyal to God's Law. This event apparently begins the canonization process by circumscribing the Pentateuch as holy and authoritative. Hence from the time of the Great Assembly at *Nehemiah* 8:4, the books of Moses were officially holy. Those and only those.

There seem to be no public ritual readings of anything except the scroll of the covenant when 'Jeremiah' (655–586 BCE) says at chapter 36:

> [1] The word came to Jeremiah from the LORD:
> [2] "Take a scroll and write on it all the words that I have spoken to you against Israel and Judah and all the nations, from the day I spoke to you, from the days of Josiah until today. [3] It may be that the house of Judah will hear all the evil which I intend to do to them, so that each one may turn from his evil way, and

---

[27] There seems to be a progression from occasional readings to a lectionary of readings appointed for synagogue and church: Deut. 31:11; Josh. 8:34; 2 Kings 23; 2 Cor. 3:15; 1 Tim. 4:13.

[28] Here Zeitlin cites Ryle (1892), Buhl (1891), Wood, Fürst (1868), Wildeboer (1895).

that I may forgive their iniquity and their
sin." ... [5]And Jeremiah ordered Baruch,
saying, "I am debarred from going to the
house of the LORD; [6] So you are to go,
and on a fast day in the hearing of all the
people in the LORD's house you shall read
the words of the LORD from the scroll
which you have written at my dictation."

It is obvious here that the words of the prophet Jeremiah have not yet been canonized for official reading in
the Temple. Yet by the time of the Qumran community, five centuries later, *Jeremiah* was considered canonical
along with other prophets.

When did Prophetical works become Scripture? On
the somewhat ephemeral evidence that the Great Assemblies were the occasions for canonization of texts
(among other business at hand?), it is probable that the
Prophets were canonized by another Great Assembly in
199 BC. The history of Samaria, just north of Judah,
may give us some help here. As a part of their religious
ritual, the Samaritan Jews never recognized any of the
biblical books except the Torah—the Pentateuch—in
their canon. The Samaritan Pentateuch has some textual
differences from the Hebrew Pentateuch texts.

That split has an interesting history in itself. From
passages in *Nehemiah* (discussed below), scholars have
assumed that the division between Samaria and Judea
so prominent in the Gospels occurred at the time of the
return from the Babylonian exile. In the 1960s, however, a trove of Samaritan papyri was discovered that
furthers our case here in two ways: It vindicates Josephus' knowledge of history and it delays the political
division between Judea and Samaria more than a cen-

tury. So please put that assessment aside. The background, as it turns out, is more complex in its politics and more definitive of the canonical formation, than that simple tale.

When the Assyrians captured the Northern Kingdom of Israel in 722 BCE, including Samaria, they took most of the people away as captives. The Assyrian practice was to mix up captive populations, forcing them to farm on unfamiliar soils and intermingle with other alien captive peoples, to reduce the likelihood of their organizing insurgence against their captors. The peoples who then were placed in Samaria were from who knew where, among a few Jewish Israelites, who either were left behind or who migrated back.

Judah miraculously held at bay Assyria's King Sennacherib (705–681) (Isa. 36–37) and survived the Assyrian invasions without deportation, although much diminished in territory. Sennacherib's successor Essarhaddon (681–669) and his son Ashurbanipal (669–627) brought Assyria to the height of its power. Then in 614 BCE the Medes sacked the Assyrian capital Assur. In 605 BCE the Babylonians under Nebuchadnezzar gave Assyria its final blow, his victory at Carchemish, giving him the formerly Assyrian vassal states. Nebuchadnezzar went to Egypt, then stopped off at Jerusalem and took home a load of silver along with the first group of Jewish exiles, including the lad Daniel. The other exiles followed in 586, when Nebuchadnezzar razed the city, including the Temple and the walls of Jerusalem.

At the end of the Jewish seventy-year Babylonian exile, Cyrus the Great captured Babylonia and sent the exiles back to Jerusalem. Here we have in succession three theories of maximizing empirical success:

- o the Assyrians, (c 740 BCE) who minimized insurrection by placing captured peoples where they could not rebel because they were subsistence farmers, tilling unfamiliar soils; little tribute from them.

- o the Babylonians, (c 605 – 587 BCE) who brought the captives and their material wealth to Babylonia, with perhaps greater productivity in Babylonia than had they been scattered, but with no tribute from the captured land.

- o The Medo-Persian leader Cyrus, (539 BCE) who sent the captured peoples back to work their familiar soils, anticipating larger tribute payments in the long run. His empire was the most powerful until beaten on the battlefield by Alexander the Great in 331 BCE.[29]

The result was that the Samaritan leader Sanballat plotted against the Jews and especially against Cyrus' cupbearer, Nehemiah, whom Cyrus sent to Jerusalem to rebuild the city wall.

By this time the Samaritans were a mixed lot. Solomon's son Rehoboam had inherited a kingdom of people whom Solomon had burdened with inordinate taxes to underwrite his spending. Jeroboam promised no relief, so that more than half seceded from the

---

[29] Alexander never ruled an empire. His death split the results of his military victories into four smaller territories with varied results of rule. Not until the Roman Empire under Augustus was there an equivalent to Cyrus' empire.

United Kingdom under Jeroboam, yielding a Kingdom of Israel to the north and a Kingdom of Judah to the south, neither of which was obedient to the LORD. Israel with its ten tribes under Jeroboam became the more materially prosperous of the two, both Israel and Judah became morally dissolute, although from time to time Judah had a king who obeyed the LORD and strengthened the fibre of the peoples' obedience, at least temporarily. The kingdom of Israel, never.

From about 740[30] the Assyrians under Tiglathpileser took captive the Reubenites, Gadites, half the tribe of Manasseh, and took them to various places. When Pekah was king of Israel the Assyrians conquered several major cities, including Hazor, Gilead and Galilee, and carried them off, as well. Sargon II took the city of Samaria itself after a three year siege. The remaining Samaritans were taken to Medea and other places.

When Asa and his successor Hezekiah, kings of Judah, realized what was happening to their northern neighbors, they instituted theological reforms, did away with idols and their worship, and gathered united the people from the hinterlands of Judah and Benjamin, and the refugees from the north, under the safety of Jerusalem.[31]

---

[30] The date is disputed.

[31] There is debate as to whether they were gathered to the precincts of Jerusalem, or whether Hezekiah might have simply annexed their territories. For a biblical account of this era, see *II Chronicles* 15ff, *II Kings* 15ff, and *Isaiah* xxx, and the Assyrian chronicles in cuneiform on clay tablets, yyyyyyyyyyyy.

After Cyrus' release the Jews who returned had trouble with this gaggle of Samaritan people who had been left behind, and had not suffered the ills of the Babylonian captivity. Until the findings in the cave at ed-Daliyeh, modern scholars assumed that the Ezra-Nehemiah period marked the beginning of the rift between Judah and Samaria. The name Sanballat appears in *Nehemiah* in this context, but nowhere else in the Bible.

The Jewish historian Josephus, however, talks about a Sanballat in Samaria two centuries later, at the time of Alexander the Great (332 BCE). Josephus must be wrong, mustn't he?! Biblical scholars in the nineteenth- and twentieth-centuries assume that they know the history better than Josephus, who must be confusing his historical facts. They knew that Sanballat lived in the sixth century and therefore he could not also have lived in the fourth century. Or could he?

Josephus was not wrong. England had multiple Henrys and Georges; France had lots of Louises. Even the United States had two President John Adamses, and two President George Bushes, and Samaria had multiple Sanballats. Josephus knew whereof he wrote. There was indeed one at the time of Alexander, several generations after the one who was nasty to Nehemiah. We know this because of some papyri found in 1962 in a cave at ed-Daliyeh. These papyri give strong evidence that Jerusalem and Samaria remained close in trade and politics, the priestly families continuing to intermarry, until the time of Alexander the Great in 332 BCE. At that time the split was extensive and permanent. That probably means that the Jerusalem Temple canonized the Prophets after the falling out between Judea and Samaria.

Roger T. Beckwith chooses a slightly different time frame for the split between Samaritans and Judeans.

> It is now known that the Samaritans con-
> tinued to follow Jewish customs long after
> the time of Ezra and Nehemiah, and that
> the schism did not become complete until
> the Jews destroyed the Samaritan temple
> on Mt. Gerizim until 110 BC. It seems that
> the Samaritans only then rejected the Pro-
> phets and Writings because of the recogni-
> tion those books give to the temple at Jer-
> usalem.[xxxii]

But perhaps it was not that the Samaritans "rejected the Prophets and Writings". They were separated from Judea politically and religiously at the time when the Prophets and Writings became officially considered ritually holy. They were not a part of the Judean Great Assemblies that declared the Prophets (in 199 BCE?) and later the Writings (in 65 CE?) holy. Hence we can speculate with reasonable assurance that if the Prophets had been canonized before the falling out between Samaria and Judea in 332 BCE, the Samaritans would have concurred with the canonization of the Prophets and might even have had Samaritan priests in the Great Assembly that canonized them. So the Judeans must have canonized the Prophets sometime after the events reflected in the Daliyeh archaeological site.

These events we know from other sources. In 331 BCE the Samaritans lynched Andromachus, Alexander's prefect in Syria, and burned him alive. In high dudgeon Alexander marched on Samaria to put down the rebellion. The rebel leaders ran for the hills with their wives, children, and important papers, hiding in a cave at ed-Daliyeh. Apparently someone double-crossed the Samaritans, and Alexander's force found their hiding place. The soldiers built a fire at the cave's mouth, drawing out the oxygen and suffocated the insurrection leaders in the cave along with their wives and children, leaving the cave to the bats, along with some pottery and the legal documents the rebels had brought for safe-keeping.

Those documents have indeed been kept safe, except for the ravages of time and microbiology, for twentieth-century perusal. They give us a picture of a close relation among priestly families of Gerizim and Jerusalem, and we have every reason to assume close ties among the lesser families and tradesmen as well, until about 230 BCE.

This may set the earliest probable date for the Jewish canonization of the Prophets, for this reason. The Samaritan cultus never recognized as Holy Scripture anything except the Torah—the Samaritan Pentateuch—as canonical scriptures. If the Aaronic/Levitical hierarchy of the Jerusalem Temple was not separated from the Samaritan cultus until after the time when Alexander the Great caused the major rift between the Judaic and Samaritan politics, the separation of cultus may have occurred when the Pentateuch was the only canonical Scripture. We may perhaps legitimately infer that the Samaritan canon remained as Torah only as a result of the timing of the Judean canonization of the Prophets and Writings.

The phraseology of written references to the Scriptures corroborates this timing. What was the Jewish canon in the first century CE, in apposition to the Samaritan canon? In "Torah, Torah, Torah: The Emergence of the Tripartite Canon"[xxxiii] S. G. Dempster gives a helpful compendium of how Second Temple Judaism and early Christianity referred to the Hebrew Scriptures:

Pseudepigrapha

Tobit 7:13, 14:5	the law; the prophets
Baruch 1:17, 21	the statutes of the Lord; the words of the prophets
Ben Sira 39:1	the law of the Most High; Wisdom of all the ancients; Prophecies

Qumran

IQS I, 3	By the hand of Moses By the hand of all his servants the prophets
IQS VIII, 15–16	The hand of Moses; the prophets
CD VII, 15–17	The books of the Torah The books of the prophets
4QMMT C 10	In the book of Moses [and in the words of the pro]phets
4Q504 1–2 III,13	your [pre]cepts which Moses wrote

Your servants the
prophets who[m] you [s]ent
and in Da[vid]

C-16   [in the book of] Moses and in
[the words of the prophets][32]

New Testament
Matthew 5:17   the law and the prophets

Luke 16:16   the law and the prophets

Luke 16:29   the law and the prophets

Acts 26:22   the prophets and Moses

Luke 24:44   the law of Moses; and the
prophets; and the psalms

Josephus wrote after the fall of Jerusalem in 70 CE, and after all three parts of the Tanach were canonized: Law, Prophets, and Writings. He gives a numerical outline of the canonical Jewish Scriptures without naming the books in each category.

Zeitlin writes that many scholars think that the canon Josephus cited included the following among the Prophets:

Joshua

---

[32] Why all the brackets? These quotations are from damaged scrolls. The scroll editor has provided his best hypothesis as to what is missing.

Judges
Kings
Isaiah
Jeremiah
The Twelve (minor prophets as one book)
Daniel
Ezra-Nehemiah (as a single scroll)
Chronicles
Job

In the third group, the Writings (Hagiographa) were the remaining four books:

Song of Songs
Psalms
Ecclesiastes
Proverbs

According to Zeitlin, the book of *Ruth*[33] would have been added to the *Judges* scroll and *Lamentations* to *Jeremiah* [although probably not as a single physical bookroll, because of the length of *Jeremiah*] to make the twenty-four.

Zeitlin himself disagrees, however, with the "many scholars" he cites above. He suggests that the Jewish

---

[33] Roger T. Beckwith suggests that Ruth would have been appended instead to the Psalms. "The Canon of the Old Testament" in *Understanding Scripture*, ed. Wayne Grudem, C. John Collins and Thomas R. Schreiner, (Wheaton: Crossway, 2012) 73. Beckwith's dates of canonizing both the Prophets and the Writings differ from those of Zeitlin. Beckwith surmises that in its final form the Tanach is "due to a single thinker living before 130 BC." 74

Bible at the time of the destruction of the Second Temple consisted of only twenty-two books, the books of *Ecclesiastes* and *Esther* being added later. Zeitlin's forte seems to be Jewish data from 400 BCE to 400 CE. He failed to recognize the Qumran texts as genuine, and reneged on the date of Daniel. (Below) But this data from Second Commonwealth sources seems to be dependable. Zeitlin holds that Josephus had in his canon the following:

> Five Books of Moses
> Thirteen Prophets:
> 1. Joshua
> 2. Judges
> 3. Samuel
> 4. Kings
> 5. Isaiah,
> 6. Jeremiah
> 7. Ezekiel
> 8. The Twelve Minor Prophets
> 9. Ezra and Nehemiah
> 10. Job
> 11. Daniel
> 12. Chronicles
> 13. Psalms

In the third group, the Scriptures, he placed
> 1. Proverbs
> 2. Song of Songs
> 3. Ruth
> 4. Lamentations[xxxiv]

Whoa! Here is *Daniel* in both instances among the Prophets, even after the canonization of the Writings! If either the "many scholars" or Zeitlin are right, *Daniel* was canonized with the Prophets during the period after 299 BCE and before the corrective reshufflings that resulted in the present arrangement. No wonder Qumran texts and their contemporaries, NT writers, use the phrase "Daniel the Prophet"! Both the Qumran texts and the NT Gospels were written before 65 CE at a time when *Daniel* may have been listed officially among the canonical Prophets. When they wrote, their Holy Scriptures was, as they say, "the Law and the Prophets". The Writings did not yet defile the hands.

The requisite for ritual holiness, and its results, may have developed later—perhaps even not until the contretemps between Priests and Pharisees. Holding or reading sacred books as a part of holy rituals defiled the hands of those who held and read them as a part of a holy rite. This concept of defilement here seems counterintuitive to those not familiar with Jewish rites. The upshot of defiling the hands was that those books which were declared holy (i.e., were canonical), which were set apart as sacred, were *eo ipso* declared to defile the hands of those who read them as part of an assembly.

> The decree of defilement of the hands was aimed chiefly against the priests, just as were most of the other eighteen decrees which the schools of Shammai and Hillel adopted in the year sixty-five [CE]. The purpose of these decrees was to make it impossible for the priests to eat the Terumah.[xxxv]

Zeitlin notes that the Great Assembly met
- o at the time of Ezra, 444 BCE (Neh. 10:1–27),
- o at the time of Simon the Just, 199 BCE,

- o in 141 BCE when the High Priesthood was given to the family of the Hasmonians,
- o and again in 65 CE to draft a new constitution.

According to the evidence noted by Zeitlin and Josephus, and also the phrases from Qumran and other Second Temple period writers, the Great Assembly would not have canonized the Prophets until a meeting of the Great Assembly either during the reign of Simon II (219–199) or even theoretically as late as 141 BCE. Either meeting would have been after the rift between Judea and Samaria, which would account for the Samaritan canon continuing to include only the Torah. The latter date (141 BCE) nudges into the time of the Qumran community, when we already have "Daniel the prophet". Simon II's Assembly in 199 BCE seems to best fit the evidence.

It appears that even though it was already considered as canonical with the Prophets, *Daniel* was at some time shifted to the Writings. *Daniel* was already defiling the hands. That is, it was already sacred, and when read in the Temple it made the hands that touched it unable to handle the *terumin*, making it unavailable for the owner of those hands to eat until they had become ritually undefiled. Hence it was not shifting *Psalms* and *Daniel* from Prophets to Writings that made the difference with the *terumin*, [34] but the canonization of the additional books that would have increased the priestly burden.

---

[34] Sometimes referred to as 'Harry S Terumin', hinting at the pronunciation.

Roger T. Beckwith, on the other hand, puts the canonization of the Writings two centuries earlier at 143 BCE, the death of Jonathon Maccabeus, because . . .

> Josephus relates that the Pharisees, Sadducees, and Essenes became distinct and rival schools of thought ... To alter the Canon after this time would have been very controversial, and can hardly have occurred. So the Canon must have been acknowledged as closed before 143 BC.[xxxvi]

Given Dempster's collection of citings, language from the Pseudepigrapha, the NT, and Qumran, and Zeitlin's evidence from Jewish sources, Beckwith's ephemeral evidence for the 143 BCE makes that date highly speculative. Zeitlin's account of the contretemps between the Pharisaic Shammai and Hillel versus the priestly *terumin,* however, should allay Beckwith's political concerns.

In 65 CE we seem to have the canonization of and the Writings. If Pusey has hit upon what characterizes the Writings, as opposed to the Prophets, it seems to be the familial nobility and/or the regnal authority of the authors.[35] Either the authors or the subject (as in the case of Ruth, David's great-grandmother) of the Writings either were in high office or were close in rank. Job may have been of the nobility. Daniel was living in the king's household in Jerusalem before he was captured, and he became the prime minister of Babylon. David

---

[35] I am on thin ice here. We know nothing about Job other than what is in his eponymous book, so assuming that he fits this category because he is in it, and Pusey has designated nobility or authority as the qualification for the Writings, would be circular logic if I were trying to prove those attributes of Job. The reader should take it with the grain of salt it deserves.

and Solomon were kings. Ezra and Nehemiah were rulers of Judea. Again, Zeitlin:

> The rabbis were of the opinion that prophecy ceased from Israel after Daniel *in the Persian period*. Therefore all the books written after that time cannot be considered a part of the Holy Scriptures. The Book of Ben Sira was written in the Hellenistic period and that was the reason for its exclusion from the canon.[xxxvii] (emphasis added)

We see here that a Persian-period *Daniel* was an uncontested assumption of the rabbis at the time (65 CE) when the canonicity of the Writings was under discussion and also of Zeitlin himself as he writes this in 1933. Zeitlin remarks that the laws of priestly cleanliness are the most complicated in the Talmud,[xxxviii] and it was on these that the canonicity of the Writings rested.

From the viewpoint of two millennia hence, it seems fatuous for the rabbis to bother discussing which books defiled the hands of priestly readers of Scripture in the Temple only five years before the Temple and its cultus would vanish. But who knew? It is the proverbial deck chairs on the Titanic.

But not quite. The deck chairs are gone for good, but the Holy Scriptures remain. The Writings are canonical, and the process of canonization may have focused the minds of the Jewish Christians, who would have observed the process as interested outsiders, on the holiness of their own latter day Scriptures. If the Writings were not canonized until 65 CE, after nearly all the texts at Qumran were written and sitting there, then theoretically a non-canonical extra-biblical second-century *Daniel* is not out of the question. But the reference at Qumran to "Daniel the Prophet" seems to contradict that possibility. One thing we can depend on: modern biblical criticism is not how Jewish canonicity was decided.

Could a late and pseudepigraphical book be considered as a book that would defile the hands? Not according to Zeitlin:

> [T]he rabbis were of the opinion that prophecy ceased from Israel after Daniel in the Persian period. *Therefore all the books written after that time cannot be considered a part of the Holy Scriptures.* … The Book of Ben Sira was written in the Hellenistic period and that was the reason for its exclusion from the canon.[36],[xxxix] (emphasis added)

We see here that a Persian-period *Daniel* was an equally uncontested assumption of the rabbis at the time of Ben Sira also (probably written in the first half of the third century BCE[x]). *Ecclesiasticus* was almost certainly written in the period between the canonization of the Prophets and before 65 CE when the canonicity of the Writings was under discussion. The rabbis were thinking of Levitical cleanliness, which they discuss in terms of "defiling the hands". This Levitical issue, which is far too complex to try to discuss here, seems to be the rabbinic way of addressing, in this case, two underlying issues. One was between Pharisees and Priests. The rabbis Shummai and Hillel issued a decree that Zeitlin says was aimed primarily at the Priests.

> The Pharisees who strongly opposed any distinction between Priests and Israelites,

---

[36] Zeitlin here footnotes Seder Olam Rabba, XXX.

> insisted that even vessels touched by the
> Priests required purification. This is undoubt-
> edly the decree of defilement of the hands
> which the Talmud ascribed to Shammai and
> Hillel... Rabbi Akiba was opposed... The pur-
> pose of these decrees was to make it impos-
> sible for the priests to eat the Terumah (the
> offering).[xli]

Apparently, if more books were declared sacred, the
priestly tummies would suffer.

The evidence suggests that *Daniel* —already defiling the
hands as prophetical—was at some time shifted to
Writings. (probably at the Assembly in 65) The other
issue, which perhaps lay beneath the political aspect of
the question of defiling the hands, was the matter of
holiness. The earliest source on record that comes
explicitly close to the three Tanakh categories found in
the Masoretic Text is the *Bava batra* 14b from the
Babylonian Talmud (after 400 CE), which has the
Prophets as

> Joshua
> Judges
> 1&2 Samuel
> 1&2 Kings
> Jeremiah
> Isaiah
> Ezekiel
> The Twelve

and the Writings as

> Ruth
> Psalms
> Job

Proverbs
Ecclesiastes
Songs
Lamentations
Daniel
Esther
Ezra-Nehemiah
1&2 Chronicles.

So it must have been some time after the early Christian period that *Esther* and *Ecclesiastes* were admitted to the canon with the Writings and that both *Daniel* and *Psalms* were shifted from the Prophets to the Writings. In keeping with Pusey's theory that kingly family or regnal authority was what elevated an author's book to the Writings, *Esther* would have qualified as the work of Mordecai, and *Ecclesiastes* as the work of Solomon.

The *Bava batra* also says, at 101,

> The men of the Great Assembly recorded/
> wrote Ezekiel and the twelve minor prophets,
> Daniel and the scroll of Esther. Ezra recorded
> his book and the genealogies of Chronicles
> up to his own time.

Should this be interpreted to indicate the it was the Assembly, rather than 'Ezekiel', 'Daniel', and the minor prophets, who authored their books? Probably not.

Perhaps the *Bava batra* here suggests that the authors were themselves members of an on-going Great Assembly which 'Nehemiah' reports as convening under Ezra (like noting that they were Members of Knesset, without saying that they were in the sitting Knesset that passed such-and-such a law). The Great Assembly may have been a rank to which one attained, even if the group had no occasion to actually assemble during one's lifetime, like the House of Lords. If you become a Bishop, you are a member, even if the House of Lords—miracle of miracles—should decree not to meet. A more popular view is that the term 'wrote' here means simply that the Great Assembly had official copies made of those books, probably as authoritative copies for the Temple.

There seems to be no evidence that an early Jewish or Christian writer had any doubt of *Daniel*'s canonicity or of its authenticity as dating from the age of the Babylonian exile. Quite the opposite. But Driver, along with many non-Jewish scholars, oversimplifies the problem of a *Daniel* canonized among the Writings rather than the Prophets. The period for Writings that defiled the hands ended with *Daniel* in the Persian period. If Ben Sira was disqualified because he came during the Hellenistic period, it becomes manifestly clear that because *Daniel* was declared holy it must have been written in the sixth century BCE and not the second century. Despite Driver, the *Daniel* scroll should be—and is—classified among the Writings.

To mistake a genuine article for a hoax is sad, and occasionally tragic. Think *Principessa*. Here is a delicate portrait by Leonardo da Vinci, and some art experts saw it as a hack's prosaic nineteenth-century exercise in the Renaissance style. Some of the world's foremost art critics could have relegated her to obscurity forever.

Think *Daniel*. Here is a masterful piece of sixth-century literature—an autobiographical trove of notes from a principal player at high-level meetings in three royal administrations, including an eyewitness account of a king's debilitating mental illness and recovery, and an eyewitness account of the precipitous fall of a vast empire. Professor Driver builds such an impressive case against *Daniel*'s authenticity that other such prominent scholars as Brevard Childs consider Driver's to be the final word on *Daniel*.

Twentieth-century archaeological and paleographical evidence, however, undermines most of Driver's case against an early date for *Daniel*.

5
Driver on *Daniel*

Oxford professors Pusey and Driver have an interesting dual role to play in our *Daniel* drama. Driver is a dogmatic porphyrist, making charges that Pusey has already answered decades earlier. But Driver lays out his objecttions to a historical Daniel so methodically that he clarifies the problems beautifully.

Pusey's style of writing is turgid, and the force of his argument is disguised by his billowy and expansive presentation. Driver's argument is crisp and clear: each problematic passage is numbered, with words and phrases italicized lest one miss the issue at hand, and then the *riposte* is set out clearly and authoritatively. I argue, however, that many of Driver's points are mistaken: he is wrong, but his very tone commands respect. He writes "for schools", and divides his analysis of authorship and dates into three easy-to-follow categories: (I) history, (II) language, and (III) theology. It is easy to see why his account is so readily accepted. Why read Pusey when Driver is so much more readable? Because Driver is mistaken. He is "Wrong Way Driver", running magnificently toward the wrong goal.

We discussed, above, Driver's concern about canonicity (his number I-1) giving it an entire over-sized chapter. His other objections to *Daniel*'s sixth-century dating are discussed here with responses mostly from other scholars.

I – 2. Jesus ben Sirach (c. 200 B.C.), in
his "Let us now praise famous men,"
([ch.] 44–49) is silent as to Daniel. Therefore the book was written after the time
of ben Sirach.[xlii] [37]

I agree with Driver that it seems anomalous that Daniel
is not in this list. At the time ben Sirach is thought to
have written, *Daniel* may even have been listed among
the canonical Prophets, although Driver would not
have known this. Mordecai, the author and hero of the
book of *Esther*, is also missing from the list. Perhaps
ben Sirach disqualified both Daniel and Mordecai
because they were writing in Persia (although both
names are listed among those who returned after the
exile: Neh. 7:7; 10:6). The biblical hero Samson is also
missing and doesn't have the Babylonian excuse.
(Gaza?) Yet each of the three saved the Chosen People
at crucial times, in obedience to the Lord. We leave
Driver's observation here with the fact that ben Sirach's
Ecclesiasticus list is not exhaustive.

I – 3. That Nebuchadnezzar besieged Jerusalem, and carried away some of the sacred
vessels in 'the **third** year of Jehoiakim' (Dan.
1:1,2) though it cannot, strictly speaking, be
disproved, is at least doubtful: not only is the
Book of Kings silent, but Jeremiah, *in the following year* (25:9 ff), as also in Jehoiakim's fifth
year (25:29), speaks of the Chaldaeans in
terms which seem to imply that their arms

---

[37]Zeitlin says 'Ben Sira' and Driver says 'ben Sirach'. Since the transcription
of the name is of no special significance, I will follow the spelling of whoever
is leading the discussion.

had not yet been seen in Judah. (emphasis Driver's)[xliii]

The simple answer is that there was a difference between the Judaic and Babylonian dating of royal administrations. But to make a short story long, here's a more complicated version.

King Josiah of Judah was killed at the Battle of Megiddo in 609 BCE. His son Jehoiakim was named king. In Jehoiakim's third regnal year, Nebuchadnezzar defeated the Egyptians (to whom Jehoiakim as vassal had been paying tribute) at the Battle of Carchemish in 605 BCE. That (609–605) looks like four years to us, doesn't it? But not according to the reckoning by the Jewish system of that time. Jehoiakim's first regnal year began not with the date of his coronation, but with the New Year after he was crowned.

The underlying question here is concerned with "What did 'Daniel' know?" If the author of the book is writing in the second century, then it might be expected that he wouldn't know his history well, and would get confused about dates and people. 'Daniel' sets the date when he himself was carted off to Babylon, along with other nobles and the Temple treasure. 'Jeremiah', though, had it differently. Which was right? Both. There was no system of international dates. Nor did they have any idea how many years Before Christ or Before the Common Era they were living. So they dated everything by the dates of the rulers. But was a king's first regnal year the calendar year during which he was crowned, or did the counting begin with the start of the first full calendar year of his rule? Would Daniel have used the Jerusalem dating system, or the Babylonian?

Joyce Baldwin resolves this by pointing out that *Chronicles*, and *Kings*, written in Jerusalem, use the Judaic system, whereas *Daniel* was written in Babylon and uses the Babylonian system for events in Babylon. Given this, there should be no objection about *Daniel's* accuracy here. So Baldwin:

> It is now well known that two methods of
> reckoning the years of a reign were in use
> in the Ancient Near East: the one most usual
> in the history books of the Old Testament
> counts the months between the king's acces-
> sion and the new year as a complete year,
> whereas the method most usual in Babylon
> called those months the accession year and
> began to count the years of the king's reign
> from the first new year.[xliv]

Baldwin, writing in 1978, can bring to bear information that was not available to Driver in 1900. The publica-tion of the Babylonian Chronicles, on clay tablets in the British Museum, made available an independent source of precise information relating to the events of Nebu-chadnezzar's accession. Although the first partial text of one of the Babylonian Chronicles came out in 1882, the principal editions of these texts were published in 1907 (L. W. King), 1923 (C. J. Gadd), 1924 (S. Smith), and 1956 (D. J. Wiseman). A comprehensive critical edition by A. K. Grayson was published in 1975. Hence writing in 1900 Driver would not have had most of this evi-dence, whereas Baldwin in 1978 would have it all.

As to whether Nebuchadnezzar's arms had been seen in Judah, Driver is right that there is no mention here of a siege of Jerusalem. At this time in *2 Kings*, though, it does say that in the days of Jehoiakim "Nebuchadnezzar king of Babylon came up, and Jehoiakim became his servant three years" (24:1) and *2 Chronicles* adds, "Against him came up Nebuchadnezzar king of Babyl-on and bound him in fetters to take him to Babylon" (36:6). It is the author of *Chronicles* whose facts are slightly askew here. It was not Jehoiakim but his successor who was bound and taken to Babylon. It is *'Daniel'* who is the more accurate on this.

After Nebuchadnezzar defeated the Egyptians in the Battle of Carchemish in the spring/summer of 605 BC, he pursued the Egyptian army all the way to Egypt and in doing so, effectively took possession of the whole of Hatti-Land (i.e., Syria-Palestine), which had been an Egyptian vassal. Nebuchadnezzar's father, Nabopalassar, died August 15, 605, and Nebuchadnezzar acceded to the throne on September 7. On his way home he probably stopped off at Jerusalem, camped his troops around the city (which would have looked like a siege to a teenaged boy), to collect Temple treasure and members of the nobility.

The Egyptian Pharaoh had put Jehoiakim on the throne, and therefore Nebuchadnezzar, in taking all that belonged to the king of Egypt, would include the kingdom of Judah. This would have been the occasion when Jehoiakim became his servant/vassal.[xlv] As for arms being seen, the military event occurred not at Jerusalem, but at the Battle of Carchemish, hundreds of miles away. But Driver could not have put all this together when he wrote in 1900, since the Babylonian Chronicles were not yet deciphered.

> I – 4. The 'Chaldeans' ('Kasidim') are synon-
> ymous in Dan. (i4, ii2, 4, 5, etc.) with the
> class of wise men. This sense is unknown
> in the Ass[yrian]-Bab[ylonian] language, and,
> whenever it occurs, has formed itself after
> the end of the Babylonian empire; it is thus
> an indication of the post-exilic composition
> of the book.[xlvi]

Here again, the publication of the Chronicles is crucial to solving the puzzle that Driver is posing here. Baldwin observes that the term 'Chaldean' is used in two senses in *Daniel*:[38] (1) to designate the peoples of southern Babylonia, Semitic in origin, who settled around the Persian Gulf in the twelfth and eleventh centuries BCE and whom the Babylonians called 'Chaldean' (5:30; 9:1); and (2) with reference to the astrology for which these people were famous (2:2ff.). But this was not a Babylonian use of the term. Though the term 'Chaldean' was used in an ethnic sense in Assyrian records of the eighth and seventh centuries, there is a complete absence of the word itself from Babylonian records of the sixth century in either of its senses, at least so far as available texts are concerned. The biblical usage is at least for now, as Driver insists, unsupported. Nevertheless, it is unwarranted to argue from silence that its use is anachronistic.[xlvii] Driver's silence has cultural limitations.

---

[38] Sometimes what seems like an accusation or a challenge is really a puzzle that could be solved jointly with a bit more information.

The Greek historian Herodotus (484–425) visited Babylon and uses the word in the second sense that Baldwin gives above (Herod. 1:181, 185). He was of course writing in Greek, and 'Daniel' was writing in Aramaic in those sections of the roll. So the 'Daniel' Aramaic usage is unsupported, except on this technicality. But Herodotus should count for a great deal: he evidences that the term was used in that sense only a few decades after the time 'Daniel' was writing, and before Driver says that it was used in Babylonia's Aramaic. Driver is arguing from silence, unadvisedly here.

> I – 5. Belshazzar is represented as *king of Babylon* (v.1ff, vii.1, viii.1), and Nebuchadnezzar is spoken of throughout as his *father*. (emphasis Driver's)[xlviii]

In this case, Driver's argument from silence is not inappropriate: The Babylonian kings list, again on clay tablets in the British Museum, is virtually airtight for this period. If Belshazzar had been official ruler of the Babylonian Empire, his name would have been on it. Hence it is not folly that allowed many scholars to assume that Belshazzar was a figment of 'Daniel's' imagination.

King Nabonidus was largely an absentee ruler, spending ten of his seventeen years in Tema, about 450 miles southwest of Babylon. The clay tablets almost seem to play cat and mouse with us, giving us a tantalizing amount of information, but not quite enough to satisfy our curiosity. The Nabonidus Chronicles say,

> *Seventh year.* The king (i.e., Nabonidus), stayed in Tema; the crown prince, his officials and his army were in Akkad

> [the capital]. … *Eighth year:* (blank of
> two lines) *Ninth year:* Nabonidus, the
> king, (stayed) in Tema; the crown prince,
> his officials and his army were in Akkad.
> *Tenth year:* The king, (stayed) in Tema;
> the crown prince, his officials and his
> army were in Akkad. … *Eleventh year:*
> The king, (stayed) in Tema; the crown
> prince, his officials and his army were in
> Akkad … , etc.[xlix]

Why don't they come out and name Belshazzar as the crown prince in question? Why not spell out the details of his royal title and be more precise about his commission? Just to tantalize us? During that long span, ca. 550–540, the effective ruler in Babylon was in fact Nabonidus' eldest son Belshazzar. Yet his name never appears here.

Without actually having the official title of king, Belshazzar enjoyed its powers, for (as one cuneiform chronicle has it) his father had in practice "entrusted the kingship into his hand"—not just of Babylon, but of the entire empire, including Egypt. Thus it is understandable that Daniel (at Dan. 5:7, 29) was reputedly offered the *third-* and not the *second-*highest place in the kingdom by Belshazzar—who was himself second. But nary a mention of the name 'Belshazzar',[39] until the discovery of a tablet in the Yale Babylonian Collection, translated and published in 1915, saying,

> In a dream …with regard to a favorable
> interpretation for my lord Nabonidus, king

---

[39] Until that tablet was translated scholars assumed that 'Daniel' invented the name 'Belshazzar'. I suspect the 1900 edition of Driver's *Daniel* may have included that suggestion, revised after the discovery of the tablet. Several other such lacunae and anachronisms may turn up from time to time.

of Babylon, as well as a favorable interpretation *for my lord Belshazzar, the crown prince.*[l, 40]
(emphasis added)

His name at last! So much for Belshazzar being fictitious.

Driver's other issue is whether or not 'Daniel' com-
mitted an anachronism when he called Nebuchadnezzar
Belshazzar's father. The precise relationship may have
been maternal great-grandfather. There is no specific
word for 'grandfather' in either Hebrew or Aramaic.
One's progeny are one's 'children' even unto the Nth
generation, and likewise one's fore-fathers are one's
'fathers'. To accuse 'Daniel' of inac-curacy here is like
accusing an English speaker of im-precision about
different kinds of snow when we have only one word
for snow in our language. Nebuchad-nezzar, as Belshazzar's maternal grandfather, was his 'father', just as
the 'sons' of Dan (one of the sons of Jacob and
patronym of one of the twelve tribes of Israel) fought
for the land they named for their 'father' Dan (Josh.
19:47), who had lived many generations earlier. Nabonidas would no doubt have preferred to be in the male
line from Nebuchadnezzar, of course, but one makes
do with what one has.

In *Daniel* 5:6f, Belshazzar's color changed, his limbs
gave way and his knees were knocking at the sight of a
disembodied hand writing something on the wall. His
mother the queen called Belshazzar "son" of his "fa-

---

[40] *The Anchor Bible Dictionary* notes numerous other extrabiblical citations of
Belshazzar, presumably discovered after this tablet was published in 1915.

ther" Nebuchadnezzar (if one translates literally) with almost mock obsequiousness. But this is also a left-handed compliment, contrasting the prince with his (and his mother's?) far more illustrious—but high-handed—predecessor.[li] To refer to the host of a banquet where guests were drinking from the ceremonial vessels of the Holy of Holies of the Temple in Jerusalem as the son of Nebuchadnezzar, who looted the Temple for those vessels, makes the moment the more ominous.

> I – 6. Darius, son of Ahasuerus—elsewhere, the Hebrew form of Xerxes—a Mede, after the death of Belshazzar, 'receives the kingdom,' and is 'made king over the realm of the Chaldeans' (5:31, 9:1, ch. 6:1ff, 11:1).[lii]

"Who is Darius the Mede in *Daniel* 6?" is a twist in the *Daniel* plot that I will not pretend to straighten out, but it will be fun to play with it briefly. Someday some scholar of Near Eastern history may come across an ancient tablet, scroll, or cylinder that conclusively names Cyrus II or General Gubaru or someone completely unknown to us as Darius the Mede.

The crux of the problem is at 9:1 when Nabonidus and Belshazzar have just lost their empire to Cyrus II the Great, king of the Medes, the Persians, and the Lydians. The text reads, "Darius, the son of Ahasuerus, a Mede, in the first year of his reign". But it was Cyrus who conquered Babylonia. Who is this Darius and how does he fit in? There is a Darius ("the First") a few generations after Daniel, but Darius the First would be anachronistic here. He is not a candidate. Of course Driver's assumption is that 'Daniel' is confused, because he is writing about events and people four hundred years earlier, and doesn't know his history.

Is the phrase 'son of Ahasuerus' an insertion by a later scribe? This solution would be problematic, because the name is in all of the earliest copies, and would indicate a both early and widely accepted interpolation. Is our under-standing of what is said about Darius' ancestry shaky here? This may be more plausible, since (as we observe above) the Aramaic (and Hebrew) do not specify gen-erations, so 'father', 'grandfather', and 'great-grand-father' all use the same word, which means any male forebear or ancestor. 'Daniel' may have known that someone—Gubaru or Cyrus, or whoever—was also called Darius, had an ancestor called Ahasuerus/Xerxes who was important enough for 'Daniel' to mention here. This is no more far-fetched than the Sanballat story below. We have several speculations to examine.

D. J. Wiseman makes a strong case for the hypothesis that Cyrus the Great and Darius the Mede are one and the same. "So this Daniel prospered during the reign of Darius *waw* the reign of Cyrus the Persian." Wiseman notes that the *waw* joining the two names, which can be translated 'and', should be taken as appositional or ex-plicative--it explains who Darius was—and can be translated as 'namely' or 'that is to say'.[41, liii] Cyrus could

---

41 Wiseman notes, "A construction long recognized in I Chronicles 5:26 (So the God of Israel stirred up the spirit of Pul king of Assyria even [*waw*] the spirit of Tilgath pileser, king of Assyria.)" D. J. Wiseman, *Notes on Some Problems in the Book of Daniel,* ed. D. J. Wiseman et al. (London: Tyndale Press, 1965), 12.

have been called 'a Mede' by the Babylonians, and as a matter of fact, he was. In 546 BC in the *Nabonidus Chronicle* of ancient Babylon, Nabonidus, king of Babylon and father of Belshazzar, declared that *the 'king of the Medes' welcomed his proposed return from exile.*[liv] (That was of course before he had any inkling that Cyrus would come back and relieve him of his empire.) Who is this *king of the Medes*? The only person then eligible for the title was Cyrus II. But that did not make Cyrus a contender for Darius, because Cyrus' father was Cambyses, and his grandfather was Cyrus I. Neither was Ahasuerus.

But there's more to this game! There is also a contingent of scholars who identify Cyrus' general, Gubaru, as Darius the Mede. Gubaru was a brilliant strategist. He had the river Euphrates diverted to an old canal, lowering the water level so that his troops could enter the fortified city by wading under the gates that were across the river. Allen P. Ross argues that with Gubaru having taken Babylon, which was considered impregnable, Cyrus must have appointed Gubaru governor.

> It is this Gubaru that Daniel calls "Darius." "Darius" is a royal title, like "Caesar," and could be applied to rulers at different levels. "Darius" cannot possibly refer to Darius I [550–486], for he did not reign until 522, long after the fall of Babylon.[lv]

If, as Ross observes, at that time 'Darius' was a royal title rather than a name, the title would seem to apply just as well to Cyrus. So Wiseman's Cyrus=Darius theory would be as plausible as Ross's Gubaru=Darius theory. We can take our pick. The Cyrus option has the advantage of a circumstantial clue regarding his age: at 5:31 *Daniel* says, "Darius the Mede received the kingdom, being sixty-two years old," a fact also noted about Cyrus. We are not told Gubaru's age. The Cyrus option has the disadvantage of having father and grandfather whose names are not Ahasuerus. We are not told Gubaru's father's name. There may be some third unknown option.

Donald Wiseman says that the description of the later Darius (II) as 'the Persian' (Neh. 12:22) could imply the need to distinguish the king of that name from one who was already known in Babylonia as 'Darius the Mede'.[lvi] Wiseman insists that his hypothesis that Darius and Cyrus are the same person is just that: a hypothesis until it is disproved or further supported by future evidence. We should note, however, that it is as well supported by data, and more explanatory, than other suggested hypotheses as yet brought to bear on this conundrum. Would that all scholars were so diffident.

Another solution here is to assume that 'Ahasuerus' is a scribal interpolation, being a scribe's historical mistake, and not the author's, just as we encountered with 'kittim' in the LXX translator's overly enthusiastic interpolative translation. (Rule 1: If all else fails, assume scribal error.)

Another creative explanation is to hypothesize that 'Ahasuerus' was another name for Cambyses, and that the fact might be clarified in some future archaeological discovery. Better yet, 'Ahasuerus' might be another form of the name Astyages, Cyrus' maternal great-grandfather, king of the Medes.

Or again, resort to rule 1. Here's a Hail Mary suggestion: The poor scribe would be transcribing it into Aramaic from some version of Farsi or whatever alphabet was used by the Medes. Unfamiliar with Median nomenclature, he may have made a mis-take and have written the more familiar 'Ahasuerus' rather than the less familiar name 'Astyages'.

Was Cyrus II (the one who conquered Babylonia) a Mede as well as a Persian? Yes, there is no question about this. Not only had he conquered Media, making him king of the Median Empire; he was also half Mede by birth: his mother was a Median princess, daughter of Astyages.

Cyrus I (his paternal grandfather) was ruler of a small, subordinate Persia within the Median Empire, which in 560 BCE stretched from Lydia and the Black Sea in the west, the Persian Gulf in the south, the Caspian Sea in the north, and the Oxus River in the east. Cyrus I's son Cambyses I, also ruler of tiny Persia, became a vassal king to Cyaxares, ruler of the Median Empire. Cambyses I married Princess Mandane, daughter of Astyages, an alliance whose fruit was Cyrus II. In 559 BCE Cyrus II inherited his father's position as Persian vassal king within the Median confederation.

As a boy Cyrus II spent much time in his maternal grandfather's household in Media. He may have detected unrest among his grandfather's subjects there. In any case, after he inherited the crown of Persia, in

550 BCE Cyrus staged an insurrection against his grandfather, Astyages, during which significant numbers of the Medes deserted to Cyrus. He won the battle and became Cyrus II, emperor of Medo-Persia. Then in 546 he set his sights on King Croesus' wealth and power, and with Lydian soldiers also deserting to his side he added Croesus' Lydia to his portfolio.

Cyrus did not use the title 'king of the Medes' of himself on any text or inscriptions as yet found. But Nabonidus, King of Babylon, used it of Cyrus. On a clay tablet for 544 Nabonidus notes that the King of the Medes approved that he, Nabonidus, was to return from his self-imposed exile. The King of the Medes at that time was none other than Cyrus II. Nabonidus no doubt lived to regret his enthusiasm. It was only five years later, in 539, that Cyrus' troops entered Babylon by stealth, interrupting Belshazzar's feast, fulfilling the handwriting on the wall, and bringing Babylonia into the Medo-Persian-Babylonian Empire. And so it came to pass that Cyrus, king of the Persians, the Medes, the Lydians, and now the Babylonians, is-sued the decree that sent some of the Jewish exiles back to rebuild Jerusalem and eventually its Temple.

The lack of any extrabiblical clarifying data leaves this question of Darius in limbo for the time being. So far as we know now, neither Cyrus the Great nor his general Gubaru was son (or grandson) of an Ahasuerus. But this might turn out to have a surprise ending like the Sanballat of Samaria drama, or *HMS Pinafore*, where a long-lost document will clarify everything, and all will be solved and fulfilled in the final act of the drama.

Prior to 1854, there were two fictional-person enigmas regarding *Daniel*. Although 'Daniel' refers to two puzzling kings of Babylon, King Belshazzar and King Darius the Mede, neither name appears in the lists of kings in the Babylonian Chronicles in the British Museum. So it was thought that the second-century hoaxer 'Daniel' must have invented both Belshazzar and Darius the Mede, being ignorant of sixth-century historical facts.

At *Daniel* 5 King Belshazzar gave a feast for a thousand of his closest friends and commanded that the gold and silver vessels that his ancestor King Nebuchadnezzar had confiscated from the Temple in Jerusalem be brought in for their use. While the guests were wine-bibbing and toasting pagan gods with the sacred vessels from the Jewish Temple, the fingers of a disembodied hand appeared and wrote on the wall

> 5 and the king saw the hand as it wrote.
> 6 Then the king's color changed, and his thoughts alarmed him; his limbs gave way, and his knees knocked together.

It was the then-elderly Daniel who was finally brought in to read the handwriting on the wall: "MENE, MENE, TEKEL and PARSIN", which 'Daniel' translates:

> 26 God has numbered the days of your kingdom and brought it to an end. 27 You have been weighed in the balances and found wanting. 28 Your kingdom is divided and given to the Medes and Persians. …30 That very night Belshazzar was slain. 31And Darius the Mede received the kingdom, being about sixty-two years old.

Cyrus came as liberator to country after country. In Media, Lydia, and Babylonia the ineptitude of the rulers caused their people to welcome Cyrus.

But 'Daniel' here doesn't say "Cyrus" but rather "Darius the Mede". In the name Darius we have an unsolved mystery. Is "Darius" another name for Cyrus? Or for his general? Or for someone else? Or, as the porphyrists would have it, are both Belshazzar and Darius pure fiction, and is this just another indication that the hoaxer 'Daniel' knoweth not whereof he writes? But 'Daniel' knows more than they suppose about Cyrus. Here is the Babylonian chronicler commenting on events next door in Lydia—events that will soon take place in Babylonia itself.

> In the month of Nisanu, Cyrus, king of
> Persia, … marched] against the country
> Ly[dia] … killed its king, took his posses-
> sions, … Afterwards, his garrison as well
> as the king remained there.[lvii]

The chronicler here discloses an issue that is one of the reasons why Cyrus can become a liberator of Babylon, rather than its conqueror. The *Babylonian Chronicle* continues:

> The king did not come to Babylon for the
> (ceremonies of the) month Nisanu, Nebo
> did not come to Babylon, Bel did not go
> out (from Esagila in procession), the festival
> of the New Year was omitted. …[lviii]

All this was happening while Daniel, a former prime minister, was still in Babylon. He would not have been oblivious to the sorry state of affairs. So next on Cyrus' to-do list was Nebuchadnezzar's empire, Babylonia, by then under the rule of the absent and unpopular Nabonidus, whose good-for-nuthin' son Belshazzar was ruling in his absence. In short, the empire had gone to pot. Like contemporary corporate raiders who have been able to take over poorly run companies and by skilled management keep them out of bankruptcy and make them viable, Cyrus was cautious in choosing his targets. The seeds of unrest in Babylonia have already been planted. By refusing to play his kingly role in the annual rituals that usher in the holidays, Nabonidus (and his son) was depriving the populace, in effect, of Halloween, Purim, and Christmas. It was as if the people of the United States had a holiday each year to celebrate the passing of the budget, and the president refused, year after year, to submit a budget to Congress. The popular holidays over which Nabonidus in his role as king presided were being snubbed in favor of his preference for his mother's Moon Goddess and his whim to stay in Tema.

Apparently there is a break in the tablets on which the chronicles are written, because it is in the

> *Seventeenth year* ... when Cyrus attacked the army of Akkad in Opis the inhabitants of Akkad revolted, but he (Nabonidus) massacred the confused inhabitants. The 14th day, Sippar was seized without battle. Nabonidus fled. ... the army of Cyrus entered Babylon without battle. Nabonidus was arrested in Babylon ... Cyrus entered Babylon green twigs [apparently the equivalent of palm branches] were spread in front of him—"Peace" was imposed upon the city, Cyrus sent greetings to all Babylon, ... the gods of Akkad which Nabonidus had made come down to Babylon ... returned to their sacred cities.[lix]

Not a word about Belshazzar, his feast, the sacred vessels from the Temple in Jerusalem, or the handwriting on the wall. Nor does the Babylonian Chronicle mention the crown prince's name. *Daniel* reads,

> 7 The king said to the wise men of Babylon,
> "Whoever reads this writing, and shows me
> its interpretation, shall be clothed with purple,
> and have a chain of gold about his neck, and
> shall be the third ruler in the kingdom."

Why "third ruler in the kingdom" rather than "second ruler" if Belshazzar was king? Just arbitrary? Nobody knew the answer until the Nabonidus cylinders were found in archaeological Babylon in 1879. One says,

> ...with regard to a favorable interpretation
> for my lord Nabonidus, king of Babylon, as
> well as to a favorable interpretation for my
> lord Belshazzar, the crown prince![lx]

How do we know this is the same Belshazzar? From this:

> Nabonidus entrusted the army [?] to his
> oldest son, his first born, the troops every-
> where in the country he ordered under his
> command. He let everything go, entrusted
> the kingship to him, and, himself, started
> out for a long journey ...towards Tema,
> deep in the West.[lxi]

The historical accuracy of 'Daniel' and his familiarity with the event is vindicated in the tiny phrase "third in the kingdom". If 'Daniel' had been writing fiction, he would have said "second" or given his readers an explanation. But everyone knew (he could assume that of his sixth century audience) that Belshazzar was second in command. Although Belshazzar was called 'king',

and for all practical purposes he was the king. He was
viceroy under his father, King Nabonidus. It was in his
power to offer only the third place, since he himself
was merely second in command.

So much for the Belshazzar issue for 'Daniel' as historian. He seems to know more about the times in which
he lived than do his modern detractors.

As for the Darius who plays such a prominent role in
Daniel 6: H. H. Rowley (1890–1969) says it is primarily
because of Darius' anonymity that he concludes that
Daniel is not a work of the sixth century BCE:

> It is impossible to believe that the mind of
> Daniel was illumined with accurate know-
> ledge of future times while, at the same
> time, thoroughly befogged as to the events
> in which he himself had played no mean part.[lxii]

Had Rowley not observed the Belshazzar finding?

> I – 7. In 9:2 it is stated that Daniel 'under-
> stood by *the books* (seferim)' the number of
> years, during which, according to Jeremiah,
> Jerusalem should lie waste. The expression
> used implies that Jeremiah's prophecies formed
> part of a *collection* of sacred books, which, ne-
> vertheless, it may be safely affirmed, was not
> the case in 538 B.C. (emphasis Driver's)[lxiii]

There are several ways to understand this passage. Driver suggests that perhaps *Jeremiah* was part of a collection of prophetic books (plural), such as *The Twelve* later
became. But we must remember that a 'book' here is a
roll. *The Twelve* minor prophets comprised a single roll
(book). *Jeremiah* is the longest single book in the Bible,

and on leather it would have been a likely candidate for bisection. twenty-two percent longer than the entire *Twelve* combined. It is not unlikely that Daniel's copy of *Jeremiah* might have been written on two scrolls—two *seferim*—particularly if they are on heavy leather. As an alternative, if we allow the *Lamentations* to have been ascribed to Jeremiah at that time, they certainly required two scrolls, explaining the plural 'books' that is a concern to Driver. Emanuel Tov notes that there is no evidence that large compositions found in the Judean desert were written on more than one scroll with the exception of the books of the Torah.[lxiv] Daniel might have had two scrolls of what is a single book in our Bibles. Or 'Daniel' may have had our *Jeremiah-Lamentations* on two scrolls.

A much-too-simple alternative is that 'books' refers to whatever collection of biblical books Daniel had. He was reading the Bible—the *seferim*—and the scroll of *Jeremiah* was included.

> I – 8. The incorrect explanation of the name Belteshazzar in 4:8 is often quoted as evidence that the writer, if not the speaker (Nebuchadnezzar), was ignorant of the Babylonian language.[lxv]

Here Driver refers to the Babylonian name given to Daniel when he arrived in Babylon. (Note that it has one more syllable than 'Belshazzar'.) Driver himself this time counters his own objection: "But possibly it is only an *assonance*, not an etymology (in our sense of the word), which is implied by the king's words" (emphasis Driver's). Driver explains in a footnote that the name Nebuchadnezzar's court has given Daniel is 'Belteshaz-

zar': *balatsu-usur = protect his life*. But at 4:8, Nebuchadnezzar says that it is 'according to the name of my god'
(namely, Bel). So Driver says that instead of etymology
the king must be referring here to what the name
sounds like—its *assonance*. It has the sound 'bel' in it.
Here Driver allows that it may have been the king's
mistake rather than that of 'Daniel' as author. (But only
if 'Daniel' is the real Daniel—otherwise, 'Daniel' has no
contact with a king to make the mistake for him. Perhaps Professor Driver has momentarily lapsed into a
belief in the sixth century *Daniel*.)

> II. The evidence of the language of Daniel
> must be considered.

Here Driver devised an almost poetic summary of his
linguistic argument that has floated down the ages of
Daniel scholarship:

> The verdict of the language is thus clear. The
> Persian words *presuppose* a period after the
> Persian empire had been well established:
> the Greek words *demand*, the Hebrew *supports*,
> and the Aramaic *permits* a date *after the conquest
> of Palestine by Alexander the Great* (B.C. 332).
> (emphasis Driver's)[lxvi]

With a set of phrases so elegantly constructed, it is with
some regret (admittedly, *schadenfreud*ian) that we find
that each phrase fails to pull its oar.

> II – 1. The number of *Persian* words in the
> Book, especially in the Aramaic part, is
> remarkable.[lxvii] (emphasis Driver's)

K. A. Kitchen makes the point that the Persian words
in Daniel are *Old Persian* words; that is, belonging to the
period long before circa 300 BCE as readily as to the

later period. Of the nineteen words here accepted as Persian in the Aramaic of *Daniel*, Kitchen tells us that eight or nine occur in Imperial Aramaic. In other words, nearly half of the Persian words in the Aramaic of *Daniel* are loan-words already attested in the sixth–fifth century Aramaic. The occurrence of four or five of them in both Persian imperial documents and Targums merely leaves the date of *Daniel*'s Aramaic where it was before: in the sixth–second centuries BCE.[lxviii] The phenomenon of Semitic and other Near Eastern words in Greek form appear as early as the Mycenaean Linear B texts. According to Yamauchi in his book *Persia and the Bible*, the linguistic traffic in the direction of Persian loan-words to Aramaic was already profuse by the time of Nebuchadnezzar.

The converse is the case with the number of Greek words in Semitic dialects, including Aramaic. Emily Vermeule accepts Canaanite etymologies for several Greek words, and Emilia Masson lists numerous other early Semitic loans in Greek in his monograph. The presence of such foreign loans—including Persian words—in Greek is evidence of considerable contact between the Greeks and the Near East long before the invasion of Alexander. In addition to such linguistic evidence, there is also artifactual evidence of early contacts.[lxix] So these Persian loan-words fail to presuppose that *Daniel* was written late.

> II – 2. [It] contains at least three *Greek* words: *kitharos, psalterion, sumphonyah* ...It is incredible that ψαλτήριον and συμφωνία can have reached Babylon c. 550 BCE.[lxx]

This objection assumes that Babylonian Aramaic would have had no Greek loan-words until Babylonia was part of Alexander's empire.

Actually, one would have thought that by the second century there would have been a much higher percentage of Greek usage in the Greek Empire, particularly under the reign of Antiochus IV Epiphanes, who made major and strident efforts toward the Hellenization of his subjects. More than a century after it was conquered by an Alexander the Great bent on Hellenizing the world, and under the rule of a man besotted with carrying out that mission, it is surprising indeed that there were only three Greek words in *Daniel*. But in fact, though, Aramaic texts for some reason fail to bear out my instinct here.

It seems that the preponderance of Aramaic texts dating from the period between Alexander (ca. 330 BCE) and Constantine (ca. 330 CE) available for study are Targums, other religious texts, internecine contracts such as land deeds and marriage contracts from the Judean desert discoveries. Literary texts, where one would expect to find borrowings *from* Greek, are predominantly written *in* Greek during this period. Taking an informal count from those included in Charlesworth's *The Old Testament Pseudepigrapha* [lxxi] we find that out of a total of sixty-seven listed works that date from the third century BCE forward, the over-whelming preponderance of them—forty-three—are in Greek and only six are in Syriac/Aramaic.

In the second century BCE, 'Daniel' not only might have used more than three Greek words, but he might have written his hoax in Greek in the first place. The author of *The Apocalypse of Zephaniah* wrote in Greek (first century BCE—first century CE). But there seems to be a paucity of Aramaic literature from which to infer any pattern of borrowing at all. There is plenteous evidence of Greek art and artisans in Aramaic-speaking and -writing cultures, but very little evidence of Greek loan words in Aramaic texts of the Second Temple period.

There are, however, only three Greek loan-words in *Daniel* to consider, and they are all musical. These Greek instrument names would have been imported along with the musicians and their instruments. Music is always international, and Greek artisans of every kind had been in Babylon long before Nebuchadnezzar. Yamauchi gives extensive evidence of Greek culture in Babylonia. He says, for example, that German excavators found cremation burials at Babylon in the area of Merkes that they ascribed to Greeks at the levels before the destruction of the city by Sennacherib (705–681).[lxxii] Greek geometric ware has been found at Nineveh,[lxxiii]

> Foreign musicians and their musical instruments played a prominent role at royal courts among the Egyptians, Kassites, Assyrians, Babylonians, and Persians as indicated by both textual and iconographic evidence.[lxxiv]

But more than that, we can speculate as to precisely when and how the musicians may have been imported to Nebuchadnezzar's court. Yamauchi informs us,

> We know that Antimenidas, the brother of the famous Greek poet Alcaeus, fought for Nebuchadnezzar as a mercenary against Ascalon/Askelon in 604.[lxxv]

From this we may be able to infer how and when some Greek musicians came to Babylon. We have evidence in ration tablets found in the vaulted building next door to Nebuchadnezzar's palace that from the Philistine city of Ascalon/Askelon (on the Israeli coast between Jaffa and Gaza, south of modern Tel Aviv) came three sailors, eight leaders, and *an unknown number of chiefs of musicians* (emphasis added).[lxxvi] Nebuchadnezzar brought them back from his trip to Egypt, perhaps the same trip in which he also brought Daniel and friends from Jerusalem. These musicians would have left neither their instruments nor their vocabulary back in Ascalon. So if 'Daniel' is writing in the sixth century BCE those Greek terms would not have been out of place. [lxxvii] So much for Driver's three Greek words' "demanding".

Do the Hebrew words in *Daniel* support a period after the Persian empire had been well established? Well, not really. W. J. Martin takes up the gauntlet on this issue. He points to a Hebrew proof-word Driver uses to claim a late usage that turns up in the books of *Numbers, 1 Samuel, Jeremiah, Nehemiah,* and *Ezra.* Martin notes, "It must have been one of the most frequently used words in the spoken language since the time of Isaiah."[lxxviii] Martin concludes that to make out a plausible case for the lateness of *Daniel* on lexical grounds, one would have to show not only that the words or idioms did not occur earlier, but also that there was *prima facie* evidence against the possibility of their appearing. Martin:

> There is no intrinsic probability that any of the terms listed could not have been used much earlier... There is nothing about the Hebrew of Daniel that could be considered extraordinary for a bilingual or, perhaps in

this case, a trilingual speaker of the language in the sixth century BCE.[lxxix]

So neither do Driver's Hebrew words support.

> II – 3. The Aramaic of Daniel (which is all but
> identical with that of Ezra) is a *Western* Aramaic
> dialect, of the type spoken in and about *Palestine*.
> (Driver's emphasis)

If as we argue here Ezra's and Daniel's careers over-
lapped, it is only natural that their Aramaic usages
would be similar. They both learned their Aramaic in
Babylonia. So twenty-first-century scholarship seems to
be pretty well agreed that Driver's case on this point is
at best unprovable, if not disproved.

Gleason Archer has made an in-depth comparison of
the *Daniel* Aramaic to the *Genesis Apocryphon,* an Aramaic
text found at Qumran that dates from the second century BCE. As noted above, this is one of the few Aramaic texts that date from the second century BCE. Driver wrote long before Qumran was discovered, and so
had no acquaintance with Aramaic texts that date authentically from that period. Archer finds that the *Apocryphon*'s Aramaic diverges starkly from the *Ezra-Daniel*
Aramaic.

> In the area of morphology, for exam-
> ple, ... the *Apocryphon* often uses … a
> form not hitherto known in Aramaic
> before the Targumic period [i.e., Ara-
> maic translation and commentary on
> the Hebrew Scriptures, dating from the
> second century BCE and forward]. There-
> fore, we find … [a class of] verbs, which
> never takes place in Daniel or Ezra, but
> is … characteristic of the Palestinian Tal-

mud and Midrashim [i.e., post 70 CE].
Archer then notes word formations in the *Apocryphon*
not found in any [other] pre-Christian Aramaic…. Archer gives example after example of linguistic changes
from biblical Aramaic (*Daniel* and *Ezra*) to the Aramaic
of the *Genesis Apocryphon*. He says,

> The only fair inference resulting from a comparison with the biblical Aramaic chapters is
> that the latter [i.e., *Daniel*] represents a stage
> of the language earlier than the *Apocryphon*…
> There are (unlike Daniel) absolutely no internal vowel passives …in the *Apocryphon,* so far
> as can be ascertained from the unpointed text
> … Its word order is distinctly that of Western
> Aramaic, rather than showing the tendency to
> delay the verb until later in the clause—a trait
> of Eastern Aramaic very characteristic of Daniel… The spelling proliferates vowel letters such
> as characterize the so-called Hasmonean orthography of the Hebrew sectarian documents from
> the second century B.C., discovered in the Qumran caves.[lxxx]

Even a reader with no understanding of Aramaic can
follow the gist of Archer's argument here, although the
article cited gives relatively few examples compared to
the more technical study he presented as the original
paper. Archer concludes that the *Apocryphon* "furnishes
very powerful evidence that the Aramaic of *Daniel*
comes from a considerably earlier period than the second century BC" A level of expertise in Aramaic that I
admittedly lack would be needed to evaluate or counter
the examples Archer offers in favor of a *Daniel* much
earlier than the *Apocryphon*. We must wonder what Driver's *riposte* might be, if any.

> III. The *theology* of the Book (in so far as it
> has a distinctive character) points to a later
> age than that of the Exile... The conception
> of the future kingdom of God, and the doc-
> trines of angels, of the resurrection, and of a
> judgment on the world, appear in Daniel in a
> more developed form than elsewhere in the
> O.T., and exhibit features approximating to,
> (though not identical with) those met with in
> the book of *Enoch* [post Maccabees].[lxxxi]
> (emphasis Driver's)

Driver continues a bit later, saying that while the determination of the date of the OT writing from its religious doctrines is always a delicate procedure, yet, as far
as a doctrinal development can be found in the OT, the
Daniel comes after all other OT writings and stands
most closely to the Jewish literature of the first century
BCE. What can one say to this? Yes! Zeitlin noted
above that

> The rabbis were of the opinion that pro-
> phecy ceased from Israel after Daniel *in
> the Persian period.* Therefore all the books
> written after that time cannot be consi-
> dered a part of the Holy Scriptures.

One must agree with Driver that theological insights
about the kingdom of God are precociously advanced
in *Daniel*. The same ideas are only embryonic in *Isaiah*
65 and 66, and 'Isaiah' is a genius, too. *Daniel* both an-
ticipates and influences the writings that come after his.
Daniel gives the world an angelology that is not equaled
until the NT builds on it.

If we are teaching *Daniel*, do we portray the writer as a
second-class hack who never had an original idea of his

own? If so, from whom might we suggest that he borrowed? [42]

---

[42] Writing as he does at the turn of the twentieth century, S.R. Driver may be in the thrall of Hegelian historicism. John Bright notes that "a reconstruction of Israel's religion … had its ultimate origin in the philosophy of Hegel as applied to the religion of Israel … [holding that] an evolutionary pattern was observable in all of human history." "Modern Study of Old Testament Literature" in *The Bible and the Ancient Near East*, ed. G. Ernest Wright (Winona Lake: Eisenbrauns, 1979) 15. Driver assumes, therefore, that advanced theological ideas cannot be part of a primitive sixth century *Daniel*.

6
Ezekiel and the
Rapha~Man Diversion

The book of *Ezekiel*, the memoirs of a Jewish priest
who was taken to Babylonia in the second wave of the
exiles, mentions a Daniel in two separate contexts.

If Ezekiel's Daniel is the Daniel in the book of *Daniel*
then there is no question but that Daniel was a historical person, and it is strong evidence that *Daniel* was
written in the sixth century BCE. But this Daniel's identity is questioned. Remember Porphyry of Tyre? He has
followers among modern scholars, to whom I refer
here as porphyrists as short-hand for someone who
assumes that *Daniel* is a second-century pseudepigraphon. They now suggest that Ezekiel's Daniel is a character in an epic poem found on buried clay tablets from
the city of Ugarit, which was destroyed in the thirteenth
century BCE.

What Ezekiel says is this. At 28:2,3 *Ezekiel* prophesies
against the prince of Tyre:

> 2Thus says the Lord GOD: Because
> your heart is proud, and you regard
> yourself to be as wise as a god—in-
> deed, wiser than Daniel—8You will
> be thrust down to the pit; you shall
> face death in the midst of the seas.

At 14:14, 20 'Ezekiel' names three righteous men:
Noah, Daniel, and Job. Jewish elders come to Ezekiel

the prophet, but he discerns that they have succumbed to idol worship.

> ⁶Repent and turn from idolatry and from
> the worse sins to which it leads, which is
> so bad that when it infects a society, ²⁰even
> such virtuous men as Noah, Daniel, and
> Job could save only themselves, and not
> the society.

Who is this Daniel? Was 'Ezekiel' writing about a contemporary Daniel, the Jewish prime minister of Babylon during the reign of Nebbuchadnezzar? Or was he writing about a character in an epic poem from an alien civilization all of whose artifacts had been buried for seven centuries?

John B. Taylor opts for the latter in his commentary on *Ezekiel*, saying that our man Daniel of the Babylonian exile is unknown in the Bible outside his eponymous book. So Taylor:

> [Daniel of the Bible] can hardly be Ezekiel's
> contemporary in exile [Why?]: in any case
> the word used here is 'Dani'el' and not 'Dan-
> niyye'l' as in the book of that name. The like-
> lihood is that this is the 'Dan'el' of the ancient
> Canaanite epic discovered in 1930 at Ras Sham-
> ra, the ancient Ugarit, on the north Syrian coast,
> and dating from about 1400 BC. [Really?] He
> appears there mainly as the dispenser of fertility
> [Oops!], but also as the upright one, judging the
> cause of the widow and of the fatherless. We
> must suppose either that this early Semitic liter-
> ature was known to later Hebrew generations
> or, more likely, that ancient Hebrew traditions
> which have not survived incorporated material
> that centred around a character of the same

name and *similar character* to the Ugaritic Dan'el.[lxxxii] (emphasis added)

Why must we suppose those unlikely options? Apparently because the alternative—that the Lord God can give one of his followers prophetic predictions—is untenable to Taylor and his fellow porphyrists. This Ugaritic Danel has become their piece of flotsam to grasp lest they drown in a sea of foolish belief in predictive prophecy.

I suggest that their belief in Danel-theRapha-Man as the referent for Ezekiel's Danel is much more foolish than believing in predictive prophecy. Such a claim is an example of parallelomania, a gambit first brought to the academic attention by Samuel Sandmel.[lxxxiii] Parallelomania occurs when, on the basis of a superficial similarity there is a derivative affinity of some sort, such as the name Danel in both the Ugaritic literature and the book of *Ezekiel*. D. A. Carson includes paralellomania among his exegetical fallacies.[lxxxiv] There is no evidence for survival for seven hundred years of either the literature or the tradition that Taylor postulates. The poem is on baked clay tablets buried underground by the destructtion of Ugarit by the Sea People,[43] and not seeing the light of day until 1929. The odds of the poem or the tradition being revived by 'Ezekiel' approach zero. I have two reasons.

First, the Jewish cultural tradition militates against the story's survival. Taylor is arguing *into* silence. Rather than saying that something did not happen because

---

[43] About 1190 BCE.

there is no evidence that it did, Taylor is saying that something must have happened, even though there is no evidence that it did, because without it the result is unaccepable—accurate predictive prophecy! Horrors!

The astute reader will, however, notice that I here am making an argument *from* silence. Either argument—into silence or from it—in can be fallacious or not, depending on circumstantial evidence. I bring evidence to show that the possible avenues for 'Ezekiel' to know about the Rapha-Man are missing—there is no way that anyone in the world at the time of Ezekiel could have known about the Ugaritic Danel. I have great faith in the academic community's fondness for the Rapha-Man as a solution to the dating of *Ezekiel*'s "Danel". If they had found a tradent from Danel-the-Rapha-Man, suplicant of Baal, to Ezekiel, exile in Babylonia, Prophet of the Lord, they would not have kept it hidden under a bushel, but would have bran-dished about the literature with gusto. I have seen no such tradent.

My second point is that even if 'Ezekiel' had known of Danel the Rapha-man, he is not the sort of hero that the prophet Ezekiel as a man of God would choose for either of these references to Daniel. Even if Taylor were successful in conjuring up a Jewish tradition that venerated a Ugaritic Daniel hidden in some of their hearts as a folk hero, 'Ezekiel' still would not have chosen him because the Lord would not have com-mended him to his prophet. Let's look at the Rapha-Man closely. Ugarit was a city on the seacoast of the eastern Mediterranean, north of Tyre, Sidon, and Byblos, roughly opposite the island of Cyprus. In 1929 French archaeologists began digging its remains at the Ras Shamra

site, occupied (though not continuously) from about
6500 until 1180 BCE and sporadically after that date.
After becoming an important trading city with a significant archive of records and texts in cuneiform[44] script
on clay tablets, Ugarit left a fascinating record of bull
and heifer idol worship and its bizarre liturgy in which
the priests of Baal have sexual intercourse with a heifer
as part of the worship service.

French archaeologists discovered a recognizable civilization on the site. Ugarit is not mentioned in the Bible,
but was already known in the literature of the ancient
near east. That civilization had begun about 2000 BCE
with the arrival of nomadic populations that, little by
little, settled in Syria.[lxxxv] During the centuries from circa
1450 - 1190, it was identifiable as Ugarit, a city not
mentioned in the Bible but known from other ancient
texts. In the moment when Ugarit's Hittite allies were in
supreme danger from an invasion of the Sea-Peoples.
King Ammurapi of Ugarit sent troops and ships to the
support of the Hittites, who were already under attack.
This left Ugarit itself defenseless, and it was destroyed
by the Sea-Peoples (whoever they were) in about 1190
BCE. The result was that it disappeared forever from
the historic scene.[lxxxvi]

In the destruction, cuneiform tablets were baked in the

---

[44] Cuneiform writing is made with a wedge-shaped stylus on a surface of
damp clay, as opposed to ink on papyrus or leather or parchment. Most
cuneiform languages use ideographs (words derived from pictures). Ugaritic
is one of the few cuneiform languages using an alphabet, with the wedges
forming groups that make letters indicating sounds, rather than stylized
pictograms as were most other cuneiform writings.

fires and buried under rubble. This was a bad thing for the inhabitants of Ugarit, but a good thing for remote posterity. Twentieth century archaeologists and paleographers found a bountiful trove of information about an ancient civilization. The unique cuneiform alphabet of Ugarit had been lost for three thousand years, along with the entire documentary evidence for that cuneiform literature.

The site was occupied from time to time during the fifth, fourth, and then again in the first century BCE, on top of the buried debris from the Ugaritic civilizations. Of course those settlements were not a continuation of the Ugaritic civilization. Their inhabitants would have known nothing of Ugarit, the destroyed remains of which lay under their floors and streets. Among the many cuneiform tablets found in the early 1930s is *The Tale of Aqhat*. Aqhat's father was Danel the Rapha-Man, who is the protagonist of the *Tale* and the persona at issue here. No one now knows whether he was historical or fictional, or even what a Rapha-Man was. Some suggest it was a tribal or family name; others that it was possibly a title or function, such as "Danel the Scribe" or "Danel the Cup-Bearer" or "Danel the King's Fool". Is he the Daniel to whom 'Ezekiel' refers?

Until the findings at the Ras Shamra site in the 1930s, mentions of a "Danel" in *Ezekiel* had been taken to indicate that 'Ezekiel' wrote about Daniel, a fellow Jewish exile who had attained high office in the Babylonian court. This was a problem for anyone who wanted to say that the biblical Daniel was fictional. So modern porphyrists seized upon the Ugaritic Danel as a solution to the *Ezekiel* problem—the problem that *Eze-kiel's* mentions give evidence of a Babylonian Daniel. Here in Ugarit was a Danel to whom 'Ezekiel' could have referred if he had known of him, and all the better that the spelling of his name in *Ezekiel* was somewhat similar to that in *Aqhat*. No matter that he was a character in an epic written many centuries before 'Ezekiel', in a different culture, and not the sort of hero for Ezekiel's purposes.

Could 'Ezekiel' have known about Danel the Rapha-Man? Not a chance. Writing about a similarity with the book of *Job* and a Sumerian poem, F. I. Andersen says that there can be no direct influence from a work more than a thousand years older than *Job*. [lxxxvii] The same is true with *Ezekiel*. There can be no direct influence from a Ugaritic poem on clay tablets buried underground for six centuries before *Ezekiel*.

Are there any elements of the *Tale* that have survived for those centuries? Yes, the goddess Anath. But she is a Canaanite goddess who was worshipped broadly. She was not a continuity of the Ugaritic literature. Karel van der Toorn notes that Anath, the goddess who in the *Tale* orders Aqhat to be killed, occurs frequently in myths and liturgical texts from second millennium Ugarit and Canaan, but that she seems to have had little importance in first millennium Phoenicia or Babylonia.

So neither the story nor its second male lead, Danel, would have come down for those centuries in the lore of Tyre or Judah. Silence reigns about Aqhat and his father Danel the Rapha-Man. The Ugaritic literature disappeared with the destruction of the city and its people, gone without a trace for all practical purposes.[45]

But both the Jewish audience-in-exile and also the prince of Tyre would have known of Daniel, the Jewish prime minister of Babylon: the prince's contemporary and superior in diplomatic rank. The prince was head of a powerful maritime city-state; Daniel was the highest-ranking official of Babylonia, the most powerful empire in the world at that time (Dan. 2:48; 6:3; 6:28).

Babylon—in the person of Babylon's prime minister, Daniel—may recently have trounced Tyre at the nego-tiating table. Daniel even may have bested him consis-tently in negotiating trade agreements for tin, copper, spices, balsam, what-all. But no matter: Ezekiel in-structs and prophesies to his exiled Jewish audience in this passage through his supposed remonstrance of the prince. The God of Ezekiel looks on pride, boasting, and claims to equality with God with mixed amusement and disgust. When we claim or aspire to equality with God, he takes us down a peg or two. Look at Adam and Eve, who merely aspired to be as God in know-ledge. So you, King of Tyre who are proud and boast-ful, you are heading for a fall! Thus saith the LORD:
Say to the ruler of Tyre, Because your

---

[45] Van der Toorn continues within a discussion of whence derived the goddess Anat-Yahu in Elephantine: "In view of the virtual absence of Anat worship in Palestine and Phoenicia, it is unlikely that the association of Anat with Yahweh (Yahu) has ancient roots in Israel. Reference to Anat-Yahu in Elephantine, then, cannot be used to prove that, in early Israelite religion, Anat was the consort of Yahweh." Karel van der Toorn, "Anat-Yahu and the Jews of Elephantine," *Numen: International Review for the History of Religions* 39, fasc. 1, April 1992, 82–83.

heart is lifted up and you say, I am a god
—I sit in the seat of gods—yet you are
not God but a man. Behold, you are wiser
than Danel. Secrets are not hidden from
you. With this wisdom you have made yourself fabulously wealthy in gold and silver.
Therefore I will loose on you the nations;
they will bring you to the Pit. (Ez 28.2-5 loosely)

Let's pretend for the sake of covering all bases that
Ezekiel had the full and undivided attention of the
prince of Tyre. Of the two seaports, Tyre and Ugarit,
only Tyre was still strong at the time of the Babylonian
Empire and the exile of the Jews. Ugarit had been under piles of rubble and soil for 620 years, give or take,
with sheep and goats grazing above its remains before
the time of Daniel, Ezekiel, and the ruler of Tyre.

Even at the time when both Tyre and Ugarit were ac
tive there may have been minimal exchange of culture.[lxxxviii] Although their languages had many similar-
sounding common words, it is unlikely that they shared
a common literature. The two languages did not have a
common alphabet. Ugaritic was written on damp clay in
cuneiform glyphs—picture-derived letters—with a
wedge-shaped stylus. By contrast, Tyre wrote with ink
on papyrus and was instrumental in the development of
the phonetic alphabet and numerals. Nicholas Ostler
tells us that "For all its thousand years of recorded history, there is no surviving artistic literature in [Tyre's]
Phoenician [language]."[lxxxix] The Tyrians seem to have
produced nothing but ship manifests, trading records,
and the system of numbers that enables the civilization
we have today. But no literature. Poor little prince, with

no nursery rhymes or fairy tales, and therefore no Ra-pha-Man.

Ugarit is not mentioned in the Bible, nor is there any evidence for it in any Israelite literature, nor for *The Tale of Aqhat* in other Canaanite cultures. Scholars have made much of the affinities between the Ugaritic litera-ture and the Old Testament, and the Ugaritic texts shed much light on the idol worship against which the Heb-rew prophets furiously railed. We know from the many household Asherot (goddess household idols) collected from recent excavations in Israel that the Jewish people continued to worship the foreign gods, despite the ef-forts of their religious leaders.

The Ugaritic texts tell us, on the other hand, much more about the Canaanite religions and the gods wor-shipped by the peoples surrounding the Jews than we can learn from the Bible. In fact, from the Bible we hear only one side of a conversation about idol wor-ship. The Ugaritic literature complements the biblical literature, helpfully giving us the other side of the con-versation. Gordon and Rendsburg discuss biblical pas-sages that puzzled us until the Ugaritic tablets were translated. They note that the ethical and moral heights of the Hebrew Bible are not found in Ugaritic literature:

> The analogies [between Ugaritic and biblical] are
> literary rather than spiritual. Indeed the
> Hebrew view is to a great extent a cons-
> cious reaction against the Canaanite mil-
> ieu. This is illustrated by the fact that bes-
> tiality (copulating with sheep, goat, cows),
> far from being looked at askance in Ugarit,
> was practiced by the adored Baal, who cop-
> ulates with a heifer as is celebrated in the

religious practices... [H]is priests reenact-
ed his mythological career, cultically. The
Bible, in forbidding bestiality, expressly
states that it was an abomination where-
with the Canaanites had defiled themselves
(Leviticus 18:24).[xc]

That fact that the priests of Baal copulated with cows
probably does not occur to most readers of *Leviticus* as a
liturgical rite, even one to be abhorred. But the Ugaritic
literature confirms that this behavior was a public cultic
religious practice. The God of Ezekiel abhors it. This is
the same Baal whose priests on Mt. Carmel failed to
make rain in their contest with the Lord's prophet Eli-
jah. Danel the Rapha-Man, a character whose most virtuous act was to worship the idols whose priests rape
cows in church, would not have been Ezekiel's role
model.

Because the Ugaritic cuneiform is the only well-known
alphabetic cuneiform, (most cuneiform writing being
derived from pictographic origins, as opposed to having
an alphabet) and because alphabets descended from the
Proto-Sinaitic or Proto-Canaanite forms, the Ugaritic
alphabet would probably also have been revised, had
the culture that produced it not been destroyed. But it
never developed to that degree. Not only the Ugaritic
alphabet but also the entire literature written in it was
buried in 1180-90 BCE with the destruction of the city.

Because of its convenience for the *Daniel* fracas, however, recent scholars have ignored this detail, and
pounced upon this literature. Daniel the Rapha-Man
has taken on a significance far out of proportion to his
heft in the ancient world. Alexander A. Di Lella, in his

introduction to the Anchor Bible commentary on *Daniel*, credits the Rapha-Man not only with being the referent for the two passages in *Ezekiel* where a Danel is named, but also as the source of all references to ancient wisdom. He quotes the couplet that tells of Danel

> Judging the cause of the widow and
> Trying the case of the orphan.

This couplet may, I suspect, be all most biblical scholars know about Danel the Rapha-Man. They cite this couplet, and only this couplet, to show Danel's upright virtue. Di Lella continues,

> Thus from early times in Syria-Palestine
> [i.e., Ugarit] the name Daniel must have
> been associated with outstanding right-
> eousness and surpassing wisdom...
> Whatever the exact link between this ideal-
> ized hero and the protagonist of the Book
> of Daniel, there is a sufficient reason to be-
> lieve that the authors [*sic*] of the book [of
> *Daniel*] knew of such an ancient worthy
> [the Rapha-Man] and were familiar with cer-
> tain stories in which he played a leading role.[xci]

What is Di Lella's "sufficient reason" that the multiple authors of *Daniel* would have known of the Rapha-Man and given their fictitious hero the name Daniel? He offers no hint.

I have searched for evidence that 'Ezekiel' could ever have heard of Ugarit or the Rapha-Man. There seems to be no record of Aqhat or Danel-the-Rapha-man in the Hebrew tradition or the Egyptian, or any other ancient culture. I have found nothing in the ancient Near Eastern literature that might make the Rapha-Man accessible to 'Ezekiel' or to the Jewish elders, or to the Prince of Tyre. So when I saw a reference to a book entitled *Ras Shamra and the Bible* by Charles Pfeiffer,[xcii] I pounced. Surely if there is evidence of a way Ezekiel of Babylonia could have known *The Tale of Aqhat* or its Danel, I would find it spelled out in such a study.

But no. Pfeiffer goes so far as to say that some knowledge of Ugaritic is indispensable to the proper understanding of the history and literature of the Old Testament.[xciii] Pfeiffer labors diligently and fruitfully to make his case, which seems to imply that until Ras Shamra was discovered and until the cuneiform tablets found there (in the 1930s) were transcribed, deciphered, and correlated with the biblical text, no biblical scholar had proper understanding of the history and literature of the Old Testament. Even so, he concludes that there is no evidence of borrowing from Ugarit on the part of Israel or the Canaanites—by implication, not even 'Ezekiel'. Similarities between the OT and the Ugaritic cultus "are doubtless the result of the common Semitic background of both peoples", as Pfeiffer suggests.[xciv]

Nevertheless, in spite of having no evidence of borrowings anywhere, to justify the 'Ezekiel' mention of the Ugaritic Danel Pfeiffer grabs the same two lines about the Rapha-Man:[46]

> It has long seemed unusual to link Daniel
> with the worthies of the distant past, but
> the Ugaritic texts give us reason to think

---

[46] Another author I thought might at least speculate as to how 'Ezekiel' might have heard of the Rapha-Man is Mark S. Smith in *The Origins of Biblical Monotheism: Israel's Polytheistic Background and the Ugaritic Texts*. But Smith here is no more enlightening than is Pfeiffer.

that Ezekiel was referring to an earlier Daniel, or Danel. *Danel of the Ugaritic texts was a
righteous king who . . .*

> *judged the cause of the widow
> and he tried the case of the orphan.*[xcv]
> (emphasis added)

Here Pfeiffer also goes with the couplet, which seems
to be the extent of most scholars' association with the
poem. But how could 'Ezekiel' have known of the
Rapha-Man as he implies, if as Pfeiffer says, "There is
no evidence of borrowing on the part of Israel or the
Canaanites of Ugarit"?

No one knows of *The Tale of Aqhat* except from the clay
tablets that had been buried in the earth for six hundred
years when 'Ezekiel' wrote and would remain there for
another 2500 years until 1930. I urge the reader to try to
think of a source—any way at all—from which 'Ezekiel'
could have known of Daniel the Rapha-Man.

Taylor asks us to assume that the Israelites would not
only have heard of Danel's plight, but would also have
admired his worship of Baal and his panoply of idols so
much that the Hebrews would have secretly harbored
his memory in their hearts, spoken about Danel the Rapha-Man on their way, and taught about him diligently
to their children, secretly admiring the Ba'alistic ritual
copulation with cows, until finally handing down this
legend to 'Ezekiel', when he has occasion to hold up
this Danel as the model of wisdom and virtue to the ruler of Tyre (at 28:3) and to the exiled Jewish elders in
Babylonia (at 14:14, 20) as a model of righteousness.

Really? We know from archaeology that the Israelites continued to hedge their bets by keeping their household idols. But the notion that they remembered the Rapha-man seems to be a set of stacked hypotheses that go beyond anything the evidence can sustain.

Danel the Rapha-Man of Ugarit has two sterling credentials for the porphyrist: his name and the fact that if he wasn't fictitious he lived before Ezekiel of Babylonia. Porphyrists have seized upon two lines of the *Aqhat* poem, as Taylor summarizes them:

> ... the dispenser of fertility, but also as the upright one:
>> judging the cause of the widow
>> and of the fatherless.

Here is the couplet again. But is this an appropriate characterization? Not if one reads the entire poem.

First, Danel the Rapha-Man is not dispensing fertility. He is begging the idols of Baal for fertility for himself. Here is a more comprehensive excerpt from the poem about the Ugaritic Danel:

> [Danel] gives oblation to drink
> to the holy ones [idols].
> A couch of sackcloth he mounts and lies,
> A couch of (loincloth) and passes the night.
> Behold a day and a second,
> Oblation to the gods [idols] gives Danel,
> Oblations to the gods to eat,
> Oblation to drink to the holy ones [idols]...
> A fifth, a sixth, a seventh day,
> Oblation to the gods gives Danel, . . .

Here Danel is simply the quintessential idol worshipper.

But Lo, on the seventh day,
Ba'al approaches with [in response to?] his plea:[47]

Ba'al is an impotent idol. But no matter, the Rapha-Man is persistent.

Unhappy is Danel the Rapha-Man,
...who hath no son like his brethren . . .
Wilt thou not bless him, O Bull El, my father,
Beatify him, O Creator of Creatures?
So shall there be a son in his house ...
who sets up the stelae of his ancestral spirits.

Please, Ba'al, O Bull El, please grant Danel fertility; grant him a son, who will be ...

In the holy place the protectors of his clan;
who frees his spirit from the earth ...
Who takes him by the hand when he's drunk,
carries him when he's sated with wine,
Consumes his funerary offering in Ba'al's house,
even his portion in El's house;
Who plasters his roof when it leaks,
washes his clothes when they're soiled—

By the hand El takes his servant,
blessing Danel the Rapha-Man . . .
With life-breath shall be quickened
Danel the Rapha-Man [. . .]
Let him mount his bed [. . .]
in the kissing of his wife (she'll conceive).
In her embracing become pregnant ...
and bear man-child to Danel the Rapha-Man.[xcvi]

Danel is not here the "*dispenser* of fertility" as Taylor characterizes him, but the *supplicant* and the *recipient* of fertility. Danel has only daughters, and he needs a son to carry on the family legacy, a son to take care of him

---

[47] Baal's appears in Danel's dream, after he worships idols for a week .

in his old age—to wash his clothes and plaster his roof. His oblations to the idols of Ugarit seem to serve their purpose, and his wife gives birth to a son, Aqhat, for whom the *Tale* is named. Where is his wisdom and his righteousness?

Later the boy Aqhat is killed, and Danel decides that the goddess Anath murdered his son because of jealousy over his beautiful bow and darts. She sent a drunken sailor to murder him. Danel mourns him for seven years, curses everything that might have had a part in Aqhat's death, and sends his daughter to avenge her brother's murder. Tablets of the *Tale* are missing, but the only evidence of any behavior that Judeo-Christianity might consider virtuous are lines that say,

> Danel the Rapha-Man ...
> is upright, sitting before the gate,
> Judging the cause of the widow,
> Adjudicating the case of the fatherless.[xcvii]

But these lines do not present Danel as righteous—they simply tell what he was doing when he took delivery of a special bow and darts that he had commissioned to be made for his son, Aqhat. In Judeo-Christianity drunkenness is not regarded as a virtue, nor is neglecting one's roof until it leaks, or wearing one's clothes when they are soiled, or sending a daughter out to fight the family's feuds.

It has been suggested that because these characteristics obviously must denote virtues of character in Ugarit, that perhaps Danel became the model of virtue in all of the other Canaanite cultures, and that his name, in oral tradition, became a byword for virtue, just as Croesus is a byword for wealth. Hence some have objected that because Danel is in a different culture from ours, he should not be judged by Judeo-Christian standards, but by those of Ugarit.

But there are two things wrong with this objection, which stems from a version of cultural syncretism. It assumes that if Danel is admired in Ugarit, he should be admired everywhere. (Heil, Hitler! If Hitler was admired in Germany, does that him universally admirable?) Ugarit's code of virtue is not binding outside of Ugarit, or even in Ugarit, for that matter. In Islam, killing one's daughter or sister because she has been raped is an act of virtue—an honor killing—whereas in other societies punishing the victim rather than the perpetrator is an act of dishonor. Israel is not bound by Ugarit's moral code, but by the LORD's.

To assume that we or Ezekiel should admire the Rapha-Man also assumes that we understand the story. Perhaps we completely misunderstand what is going on here. Written communication obscures the twinkle in a poet's eye, especially in a lost form of writing, a lost language, a lost culture, and more than three thousand years separating us from the poet.

So I wonder if someone may have been pulling someone's leg. If so, the sentence "I wonder if someone may have been pulling someone's leg" if it were in the Ugarit language would itself be incomprehensible if translated literally. We may be reading the Tale as "King Arthur", when it should have been read as "Mickey Mouse" or "Til Eulenspiegel".

The possibility that *The Tale of Aqhat* might be a farce

seems not to have entered the scholarly discussion. If this Ugaritic epic poem is not making fun of Danel, a lazy, good-for-nothing Ugaritic coward, then Goofus, Mr. McGoo, and Til Eulenspiegel[48] are all versions of Superman. Humor is hard to translate, because it is often culture-specific and even date-specific. The lyrics to the song "I've Got a Little List" from Gilbert and Sullivan's *Mikado* must be rewritten for nearly every production, if they are to have the bite of the original. And that is in English for an English-speaking audience! So Danel begs the gods for a son to plaster his roof. He should call Angie's List. If you don't think that's a laugh line, you should try it in Ugaritic. Poor Rapha-Man. Whoever *he* was. Or who*ever* he was, I suspect Charlie Chaplin, Jim Carrey, or Rodney Dangerfield might have played Danel well.

On the other hand, we should also consider the possibility, which academia seems to hold as dogma, that Danel should be played straight: that Ugaritic society really did admire this Danel. Gordon and Rendsburg paraphrase the description of Danel as "the heroic king Daniel, who ruled his people justly and protected the widowed and fatherless."[xcviii] (Here's our couplet again.) There is nothing in the *Tale* that tells us that Danel was a king, nor that he ruled anything justly. He ruled on matters of importance to helpless people, because he sat in the gate—an honor of sorts in ancient Near Eastern societies. Simon Parker points out that Lot was in a similar situation when the two visitors arrived in Sodom, that is, sitting in the gate (Gen. 19:1).[xcix]

---

[48] All are hilarious fictional bumbling idiots.

If Lot sat in the gate at Sodom, it is an honor not devoutly to be desired. The very act of sitting in the gate would have implied that Lot, too, adjudicated the case of the fatherless (and anyone else who brought a case before the elders in the gate). It was a privilege to sit in the gate, whether the gate was of Sodom or Ugarit or Jerusalem. But it guarantees a virtue only relative to one's culture. Sodom? Hmmm. Ugarit? Perhaps not far behind. Copulating with cows in church! What else?!

Enough of Aqhat, and forget Hilary's damn emails (or whatever is in the headlines when someone reads this). Let's now see about the Jewish idol worshippers. At chapter 14 'Ezekiel' prophesies against some elders of Israel in exile who take idols into their own hearts and by doing so set a stumbling block of iniquity before their own faces:

> [6] Say to the house of Israel, Repent and turn away from your idols, and from all your abominations. [7] Anyone who separates himself from me, taking idols into his heart ...[8] I will set my face against that man ...[13] When a land sins against me, ... I stretch out my hand against it, [14] even if Noah, Dan'el, and Job were in it, they would save only their own lives by their righteousness... [20] Even if Noah, Dan'el and Job were in it, as I live, says the LORD God, they would deliver neither their sons nor daughters; they would deliver only their own lives by their righteousness.

God does not suffer fools gladly. Would he forgive the idol-worshipping elders if they repent? Yes. But would he look the other way if instead of repenting they chose to wallow in their idolatry? What did he just say?! Even Noah, Daniel, and Job's coattails are not stout enough to pull anyone else out of idolatry, which is among the worst kinds of tomfoolery.

Idolatry is a conscious rejection of the sovereignty of the Most High God. It is passing strange to suggest that Ezekiel would prophesy against these elders of Israel who have lapsed in turning to idolatry, by holding up as an exemplar Danel the Rapha-Man, whose claim to virtue is his exemplary idolatry. I can only surmise that scholars who suggest the Ugaritic Danel as an alternative to Daniel of Babylon are either not paying close attention, or they choose any alternative to the referent of Ezekiel's Danel rather than stomach the notion that God could work through his man Daniel.

Did Ezekiel know Daniel? Of course. But his knowledge of Daniel was probably like my awareness of Dr. Jonas Salk, inventor of the polio vaccine, or Billy Graham, the famous evangelist. Of course I know of them both and admire them, but the esteem in which I hold them is admiration, not friendship. Ezekiel did not even know how to spell Daniel's name: he left out the 'yod', like the American frontiersman, Dan'el Boone. Pusey notes that

> All eyes would have been fixed upon Daniel, the more marvelous his rise at that early age from being a captive boy, though of royal blood, to be ruler over the whole province of Babylon, and chief over the chiefs of all the Magi of Babylon.[c]

Did Ezekiel include our Daniel, or Danel-the-Rapha-Man, in the trio "Noah, Dan'el, and Job" (14:14 and 14:20) Harold H. P. Dressler argues, as I do here, that the character of the Ugaritic Danel would make him an unlikely match for Noah and Job.[ci]

Who are these three heroes? Taylor struggles to put Danel-the-Rapha-Man there, despite the problem he notes that "Daniel alone [of these three] is unknown from the Bible."[cii] (Danel-the-Rapha-Man, yes, but Daniel is not unknown.) Baruch Margalit, in a reply to Dressler, claims that he himself has found the key to their commonality. Margalit posits that what links the three are that *none are Jewish and all are ancient*.[ciii] Therefore Daniel of Babylon is automatically ruled out. He was neither ancient nor goyish. Ginsberg agrees, assuming that Daniel the Rapha-Man was a king, who

> was not remiss in
>
> > "judging the cause of the widow,
> > adjudicating the case of the fatherless."
>
> The prophet Ezekiel (14:12 ff) ...keeps reiterating that under such circumstances not only Noah, Daniel and Job would save either a son or a daughter... Obviously his Daniel ...is like Noah and Job, a saint of hoary antiquity, and consequently belongs to mankind as a whole. His identity with the [Ugaritic Danel-the-Rapha-Man] is highly probable.[civ]

But Ginsberg's and Margalit's assumption is flawed in more than one way. Of the three, only Noah is unquestionably not Jewish, since he predated Abraham. And only Noah is unquestionably ancient.

We know nothing of Job's origins and family background, nor of his dates. Some scholars assume *Job* predates all the other books of the Bible. Others, such as Momigliano, say that Job is among the last. But the book gives few hints as to its origin, other than paleography. Most who make the claim that it antedates other books date the other books quite late. But even if we knew that Job was not Jewish, the further inference that the Daniel here cannot be Jewish is to argue in a circle: 'They must all be goyim, because Noah and Job are goyim, so Danel here must be goyish because they must all be goyim.'

Francis Andersen suggests that linguistically the book of *Job* may be post-exilic, although Job's mention in *Ezekiel* provides evidence that Job was known during or before the Babylonian exile so as to be in Ezekiel's purview.[cv] Frederic Raphael has *Job* as "one of the latest in the canon".[cvi] Arnaldo Momigliano says, " ...the Book of Job, probably an exilic work,"[cvii] hence contemporary with Daniel and Ezekiel.

Marvin H. Pope, along with perhaps the preponderance of modern scholars, says that the seventh century BCE seems to be the best guess for the date of *Job*,[cviii][49] while other scholars maintain that *Job* is the most ancient of the canon, antedating the Pentateuch.[50] Pope argues that the recovery of a Targum of *Job* from the Qumran caves indicates that *Job* must have been in circulation for some time before the first century BCE; and while the completed book may be as late as the third century BCE (a suggestion which requires redating *Ezekiel* as well, and a wide discrepancy indeed) it may also be sev-

---

[49] Where Raphael also places *Daniel* (68–69 BCE). Raphael gives no rationale for either dating.

eral centuries earlier.[cix] We may gather from this discussion that the date of *Job* is in contention and cannot be a major factor in determining the intention of 'Ezekiel' in this passage.

If there were a Ugaritic tradition marching down the centuries of Israelite culture, surely some porphyrist scholar would have unearthed and touted it. I am counting on them here to have done so, having tried it myself to no avail. But no, Ugarit was razed, burned, and buried, and any Ugarians who survived were sold into slavery. With it disappeared the Ugaritic alphabet and literature[cx] including *The Tale of Aqhat*. An oral tradition within the Jewish culture preserving the Ugaritic 'Danel' is so unlikely that it can be ruled out for any use by God's prophet Ezekiel.

But is there a reason to link our Daniel of Babylon to the other two men, Noah and Job? Yes, several.
- They are all three biblical.
- They are all three righteous men, recognized for their godliness by traditional Jewish standards.
- They all worshipped the God of Israel, even if Noah is thought to have done so precociously.
- They were all three social and theological mavericks: they followed the LORD's leading in spite of the scorn of those around them.

Danel the Rapha-Man exhibits none of these virtues. The use of these three by 'Ezekiel' implies to anyone that no matter what his or her situation, "You, too, can be righteous. Leave your idols. Stand with the LORD!" Good-bye, Rapha-Man.

7
Prophecy

Is predictive prophecy ever acceptable in objective discussion? Many would say that it is not—that it is one of the impossible things that Lewis Carroll's Queen had had to practice believing before breakfast—quite outside the realm not only of rational thought, but outside of polite conversation altogether. Among polite twentieth century theologians and properly trained clergy, the phrase is almost a contradiction in terms: "Prophets don't foretell, they forth-tell."

But that is not how the Bible sees it. That being the case, John Oswalt gives us an insight into the problem:

> At the outset, I want to insist that we not rule out the possibility of divine revelation *a priori*. If we do that, then we have … accepted in advance the thing the Bible says is not so. So we must begin by allowing the possibility that God is not the cosmos[51] and that if he is to communicate with us, it must be by direct revelation …[cxi]

Many scholars in the present discussion have done precisely what Oswalt cautions against: they have assumed *a priory* that divine revelation is impossible. "Don't bother me with the evidence, I've made up my

---

[51] Nor a part of it, nor anything except its creator and preserver with complete power and sovereignty over everything that is, was, and is to come.

mind. *The Guardian*—or *The New York Review of Books*—
says it, I believe it, and that's that." Rednecks driving
pick-em-up trucks with gun racks have no monopoly
on closed-mindedness. But not us! Surely any reader
who has read thus far is at least open to a discussion on
the subject of predictive prophecy.

If it is magic and fortune-telling and Delphic Oracles
you have an aversion to, count me in. Accurate predict-
tive prophecy requires a God who is maker of heaven,
and earth, and of all things, visible and invisible: the
God who is sovereign over all creation. Anyone who
cannot accept such a God cannot logically accept predictive prophecy. And conversely, anyone who accepts
such a God must be open to the proposition that God
can predict what He will cause to happen in the future
of his creation and can also authorize one of his created
beings to tell the world about it. If God could not
control the future, he would not be able to predict the
future, to say nothing of not being able to tell the future
to his prophets. But the God of creedal Christianity
does control past, present, and future. God is sovereign
over everything, causing every vibration of every
atom—"all things, visible and invisible."

Well, if he is all-powerful and all-good, why is there evil
in the world? Why do innocent children get cancer and
die? Why do perfectly nice people get caught in torna-
dos or buried in mud slides?

God only knows, and he is not only not obligated to
explain everything to us, but we are incapable of
understanding the 'everything' over which God reigns.
Think of trying to explain to your dog why he needs to

take a pill or why you are leaving and when you are coming back. He doesn't understand. And I didn't even create my dog. God is approximately $10^{5,000}$ times more intelligent than I am, and I am a fraction of that more intelligent than my dog. That's just a rough estimate, of course. The precise ratio depends on my IQ and that of my dog, both of which are iffy. God is not iffy. He founded and operates the whole business—earth, stars and cell membranes.

God creates our brains. Francis Collins, the director of the human genome project and now director of the US National Institutes of Health, tells us that there are eighty-six billion neurons in our brain, each of which has about a thousand connections.

> The complexity of this structure exceeds
> anything else in the known universe, and
> some have worried that our brains are not
> complicated enough to understand our brains.[cxii]

That makes perfect sense to me, because of Gödel's incompleteness theorems, which I also don't understand. I cannot run a four-minute mile, either. I have come to accept that I cannot wrap my body around a four-minute mile, cannot wrap my brain around Gödel's theorems, and if Collins hypothesizes that our brains are so complex that our brains cannot comprehend themselves, I am inclined to suspect that Collins is right. God made our brains, along with everything else. So we are wrong when we think God owes us an explanation of how or why he knows the future. He knows just what is going to happen, because he is creating every instant and causing it to happen. Do we think we would be able to understand the answer if he told us how? Does Chip understand why we sometimes put pills in the back of his throat so that he swallows them in spite of the fact that pills don't taste like treats? We could explain to our dogs in complex detail that we are going to the super market, and why, and we would still get a soulful expression from them.

If only we were as accepting and trusting of God when he does something we don't understand, as our dogs are accepting of us. We need to wag our tails in the form of singing a psalm of thanksgiving and figure out some way to lick God's hand and lie down on his feet. Dogs are probably better at understanding us than we are at understanding God. God understands us perfectly and completely because he made us. And we can understand him as far as he gives us grace.

We reveal ourselves by what we do. A concert pianist may reveal himself by the way he plays Chopin or Mozart; a juggler by juggling; a dancer by dancing. God reveals himself, among other ways, when he calls his shots and makes them, showing us his sovereignty over future events. It's somewhat like Babe Ruth pointing to the part of the field where he is going to put his next home run, or a master pool player calling the pocket where he is going to put a particular ball. God is not putting a hand to his forehead and dramatically making a prediction out of nothing. God reveals part of himself to us in the form of predictions because he causes them to come true.

For us, future is future. Our time is like an ever-rolling stream that bears all its sons away, flying forgotten as a dream flies at the opening day. Our stream of time flows in one direction only, and we have no control over it. [52] Trying to stop the flow of time is even more unthinkable than trying to stop the flow of the tides. But for God, time is something like a symphony he is composing. He can decide what the flute is to do at such-and-such a measure in the second movement and write the tympani into the last few bars of the first—but God does it simultaneously and sees the thing as a multidimensional whole. He speaks it into existence. We experience his symphony as only one instrument in the few bars of our lifetime. We perceive the rest as harmony, history, and unwritten future. But God can pause it, rewrite it, or whatever he chooses. That's not a very good analogy, but God is unique and beyond analogy.

So back to the future. The 1968–1971 television comedy *Rowan and Martin's Laugh-In* had a segment called "News—Past, Present and Future". In 1969 the "News of the Future" included an announcement that ***in 1989 East Germany would tear down the Berlin Wall***, a physical wall that in 1969 kept residents of the Commu-nist sector of Germany from escaping into the West to find political, economic, and religious freedom. That prophecy was fulfilled. The official date of the fall of the Berlin Wall is November 9, 1989.[cxiii] Other Future News that day included the announcement that California Governor Ronald Reagan would leave his brain to science. That was not fulfilled, as far as I know. But if the Lord could give accurate predictive prophecy about the Berlin Wall unto the pens of the writers of

---

[52] From the hymn "O God, Our Help in Ages Past" by Isaac Watts.

Laugh-In, who is to say that he cannot give it to his man Daniel? How many events in "The News of the Future" over the run of the show the writers accurately predicted, I don't know. I just happened onto this one. Just as a broken clock is correct twice a day, the writers of *Laugh-In* were bound to be right once in a while, and were not prophets of God by any stretch.

Many scholars maintain that *Daniel* is a pseudepigraphon—a false writing—composed during the second century BCE as a thinly disguised commentary on the oppressive government of Antiochus IV Epiphanes, while veiling it as a sixth-century work written during the Babylonian exile. Other scholars say that *Daniel* was written by many people at many times, and the compiler was a second-century political commentator. Yet other scholars argue that the work is genuine sixth-century writing, accurate and historical. Perhaps it requires a peculiarly twisted mind, but for some of us, sorting out this kind of contretemps can be even more fun than a fictional murder mystery.

This is what the Bible has to say about these situations. At *Deuteronomy* 18:10, the LORD says through 'the Deuteronomist' (aka Moses), "There shall not be found among you anyone who ...practices divination, a soothsayer, or an augur". Some would understand from this that there should be no foretelling of the future. But obviously that is not what the LORD means, because just a few lines later (18:18) he says,

> I will raise up a prophet like you [Moses] from among their brethren; and I will put my words in his mouth, and he shall speak in my name; I myself will require it of him.

So far, so good for forth-telling, but here is no obvious foretelling as yet. As long as God's mouthpiece lives, he can say whatever he probably would describe as "I felt led to say".

But how can the people tell whether it was actually the Lord who led him to say it? In some cases the person who claims to prophesy is not the Lord's chosen mouthpiece. As we all know, what some people erroneously think they are "led to say" can be pretty loosey-goosey. Without a good dollop of fear and awe, some people can feel led to say just about anything. But wait!

> The prophet who presumes to speak a word in my name which I have not ordered him to speak, or who speaks in the name of other gods, that same prophet shall die. (18:20)

Suddenly loosey-goosey has consequences. If the leading of some would-be mouthpiece is not of the LORD, and that person speaks anyway as if from the LORD, that person is in trouble: he shall die.

Will he be struck down on the spot like Ananias and Sapphira in *Acts* 5? Not necessarily. Throughout the Bible we see false prophets[53] (i.e., not of God) who live to prevaricate another day. So what should we take this

---

[53] Tessa Rajak says that the term 'false prophet' gained currency in Hellenistic Judaism (ca. 300 BCE–300 CE), though not employed in the Hebrew Bible. *Josephus*, 2nd ed. (London: Duckworth, 2002), 90. Perhaps she considers *Deuteronomy* to date from the Hellenistic period. Or she is pointing out that the term 'false' is not used here, but that the Hebrew circumlocutes. Surely the notion of 'false prophet' seems very clear in the *Deuteronomy* passage under discussion.

to mean? That God is just bluffing? That he is power-less to carry out his judgment? Or that he is so full of loving-kindness that he never fulfills his judgments? It's dangerous to think any of this nonsense! Remember Ananias and Sapphira!

"Surely die" probably means that they will no longer enjoy God's fellowship—that goodness and mercy will not follow them all the days of their lives, and they will not dwell in the house of the LORD forever. For them death, when it comes, will be sheer hell. Their presum-ing to speak as if from God when he has not com-manded them to speak has consequences. It means that Satan already has them in his clutches, and they will choose to sink more and more deeply into his clutches and further and further away from God. So we find that if the would-be mouthpiece of the LORD doesn't have some evidence of God's prophetic credentials, no one should believe him. And it turns out that foretelling is the means by which we, the people, are authorized to judge whether or not someone is a true mouthpiece of the LORD:

> And if you say in your heart, "How may we know the word which the LORD has not spoken?"—when a prophet speaks [supposedly] in the name of the LORD,—*if the word does not come to pass or come true, that is a word which the LORD has not spoken*; the prophet has spoken it presumptuously, *you need not be afraid of him.* (Deut. 18:21–22, emphasis added)

Not afraid *of* that false prophet. But we need to be afraid *for* him, because his eternal life, his very soul, is in peril. Thus the criterion for a genuine mouthpiece is that this person's prophecies come to pass. It is only with foretelling that both the prophet and the prophet's audience get unequivocal feedback.

Look at Moses. If the angel of death had not passed over all the doorposts covered with blood, and only the doorposts covered with blood, then the children of Israel would have known that Moses was not a true prophet, and they needn't have bothered to follow him out of Egypt. If fifteen more years were not added to Hezekiah's life, Isaiah would not have had his credentials certified. If Daniel had not been able to tell Nebuchadnezzar the content of his dream before he interpreted it as future empires, he would not have demonstrated that his understanding came from God—as he himself says at *Daniel* 2:27–29.

It appears that the LORD gives a genuine prophet several occasions for are-they-or-aren't-they short-term prophecy tests perhaps comparable to a bar exam or a doctoral candidate's written and oral exams that show the prophet and his audience his obedience to the LORD (not to proclaim anything that is not of the LORD) before he feeds his mouthpiece any long-term unverifiable prophecies of the future.

What about faking it correctly? What if I claim to have prophesied an event that happened this week? "Oh, I said all along that Islamic fanatics would fly planes into the World Trade Center," or "My father predicted that Bernie Madoff was running a Ponzi scheme that would go bankrupt." A judiciously faked letter to that effect dated before the event occurred would "prove" those predictions occurred. That would be prophecy-after-the-event or *vaticinium ex eventu*.

J. A. T. Robinson points out that before-the-fact bibli-cal prophecy tends to be fuzzy and indistinct. The true prophets see things as in an ancient looking glass, dim-ly, whereas the hoaxers who write about a past event *as if* it were in the future actually show the event face to face, as if it happened only yesterday (which it did).

Robinson is arguing that the entire NT was written before 70 CE. He discusses this distinction with respect to gospel parables which seem to prophesy the fall of Jerusalem, within the context of whether they were written before or after the events of 70 CE. The king was angry, and having sent his armies, he destroyed those murderers and burned their city. So Robinson:

> If Matthew 22.7 did reflect the happenings
> of 70 [after they had already happened] one
> might expect that it would make a distinction
> that features in other *ex eventu* 'visions',
> namely that while the walls of the city were
> thrown down, it was the temple that per-
> ished by fire.[cxiv]

Robinson contrasts this with *vaticinium ex eventu*,

> Thus the Jewish apocalypse II Baruch
> clearly reflects the fall of Jerusalem to
> the Romans, though it purports to be the
> announcement to the prophet Baruch of
> a coming Chaldean invasion. [So Baruch:]
> *We have overthrown the wall of Zion and we have*
> *burnt the place of the mighty God.* (7:1)
> *They delivered ...to the enemy the overthrown wall,*
> *and plundered the house, and burnt the temple.* (80:3)

Robinson says that if we really want to see what *ex eventu* prophecy looks like, we should turn to the

Sibylline Oracles, which are thought to be from Jewish sources in Alexandria, second century BCE to fifth century CE:

> And a Roman leader shall come to Syria,
> who shall burn down Solyma's [Solomon's]
> temple with fire, and therewith slay many
> men, and shall waste the great land of the
> Jews with its broad way (4.125–7)."[cxv]

Unlike these sharp-focus photographs, which distinguish burnt temple from not-burnt city, the view of the future rough-sketched by 'Daniel' is misty and shrouded indeed.

Consider the interpretation of Nebuchadnezzar's dream (Dan. 2). Nebuchadnezzar has forgotten the dream. So before interpreting, an interpreter must say what the dream was. His magicians cannot do that, but Daniel says that his God will do it:

> [28] There is a God in heaven who reveals
> mysteries, and he has made known to
> King Nebuchadnezzar what will be in
> future days. ... [31] You saw, O king, a
> great image. ... [32] Its head was of gold,
> its breast and arms silver, its belly and
> thighs bronze, [33] its legs of iron, and its
> feet a mixture of iron and clay... [34] Then
> a stone was cut out, but not by human
> hands, and struck the image on its feet
> and the whole image collapsed, disinte-
> grated, and wafted away, [35] But the stone
> became as a great mountain and filled
> the whole earth.

If the four parts of the image represent Babylon, Medo-Persia, Greece, and Rome, then Jerome is right and *Daniel* has authentic predictive prophecy. These four empires followed one another in succession. Nor did it occur to Jerome that *Daniel* might be construed otherwise, except as Porphyry choses to malign both Jews and Christians by misconstruing 'Daniel', apparently led by scribal insertions in Greek translations of the book.

If *Daniel* were written by one of the second-century writers, the identity of its pseudepigraphical author would probably have been an open secret. What we call pseudepigraphy seems to have had a similar niche in Seleucid Coelo Syria (i.e., second-century BCE Israel under the Seleucid Empire) as our science fiction has today, the best of which is not only a form of predictive prophecy, but also a veiled commentary on the less-than-sterling aspects of our own society. We like our science fiction authors. We know who they are, generally, even those who use a *nom de plume*. I suspect they knew their pseudepigraphers, of which there were several, but 'Daniel' was not among them.

The issue at hand is whether the *Daniel* manuscripts found at Qumran were a clever contemporary *roman à clef* or the classical four-hundred-year-old historical memoir of a statesman who left his testament for posterity. We see myriad reasons why it must have been the historical memoir, and could not have been the clever *roman à clef*. But despite the problems with their case, porphyrists seem loath to throw in the towel.

The moral to this story: If you plan to prophesy, either use vague, ambiguous language, or document your prophecy carefully, with a notarized document or a date-stamped video.

8
The Army of Experts

Years ago I sat in on a course for lay people about the New Testament. The textbook, in its introductory background, gratuitously brings up the subject of the Old Testament book of *Daniel* and says that "The book is pseudonymous and is written at the same time as the events it purports to predict."[cxvi] I differed, and objected to its needlessly bringing up the issue when it had very little to do with a study of the NT.

I brought the instructor a copy of Joyce Baldwin's commentary on *Daniel* from the Tyndale Old Testament Commentary series and pointed out to him that this evaluation of *Daniel* is not a consensus of scholars. He handed back the book, saying he didn't need to read it. Baldwin is wrong, he said: "All the best scholars are agreed" that *Daniel* is second-century pseudepigraphy. He was right in claiming that the army of scholarly experts in mainline seminaries—the dean's ninety-seven percent—agree with one another that *Daniel* is a pseudepigraphon from the second century BCE. That is to say, it is a hoax.

But this logic is faulty. To assume that "all the best scholars are right" based on their overwhelming numbers is to commit the bandwagon fallacy, also called the teenager fallacy: ("But Dad, everybody gets to drive after midnight.") The overwhelming numbers do not mean that "all the best scholars" are right. They often are wrong. Nor does it mean that they are wrong this time. They may in fact be right on a particular issue. Socrates says somewhere (*Cratylus* 437d?) that "We cannot put the truth to a vote."

I have read somewhere that ninety percent of great scientists start out accused as scientific heretics— Galileo, Copernicus, Mendel, Einstein, to name only a few. But merely agreeing or disagreeing with the current experts does not guarantee that a particular theory is either right or wrong. Ninety percent of the scientific heretics really are just talking nonsense. Years later, when I encountered the dean's ninety-seven percent of authors on his walls of books, I already knew that I was a theological deviant. I was at his seminary to find out whether I was in the nonsensical ninety percent, or the insightful ten percent. In the dean's bookshelf, he estimated that only three percent were deviant, but did not correlate that with ultimate correctness—quite the opposite.

Yet not even all of the insightful ten percent are vindicated during their lifetimes. Alfred Wegener published his theory of continental drift in 1913. When he died in 1930, few scientists had accepted the bizarre idea that continents could move like rafts. Not until the 1960s, with the discovery of plate tectonics, was Wegener's theory recognized as correct.[cxvii]

So even if I am right about the academic legends in biblical theology, *Daniel* may not be vindicated in the eyes of the academic community until after I die—or never. What assurance was there that the *Principessa* would be identified? The burden of proof and the vindication thereof varies. In science, the proof may be eventually unequivocal. Einstein was vindicated when measurement instruments improved and the right astronomical event could be measured more accurately than heretofore.

For historical events, such as we have here with Daniel, or as we have in a court of law, we often must make do with informal probability, or whatever the members of our jury choose to believe. What is the more likely of the alternatives before us? We must build our case a segment at a time, and demonstrate the improbability or impossibility of any opposing false or highly improbable evidence. Is it legitimate to dismiss the possibility that Alexander the Great saw *Daniel* at the Temple in Jerusalem, simply because the only mention of the event is in Josephus? Is it legitimate to proclaim the portrait of the *Principessa* a fake simply because it is unlikely that a new Leonardo might be found?

The reader has already met a goodly number of experts who land on either side of this *Daniel* dispute. Here are several more. John J. Collins (b. 1946) says,

> [T]here is a discrepancy between the surface impression gained by a practical reading and defended by conservative scholarship and the understanding proposed by modern critical scholarship... The impression that Daniel was the author of the book is derived from the first-person accounts in chs. 7–12 and the direct address of the angel in 12:4... By contrast, modern scholarship has held that Daniel is a legendary figure, that the stories in chs. 1–6 are no older than the Hellenistic period, and that the revelations in chs. 7–12 were written in the Maccabean period.[cxviii]

Here Collins stands firmly with modern scholarship. Obviously he is among the dean's ninety-seven percent.

If these scholars were right in claiming that *Daniel* could not have been written before the events it describes, then it is a bit strange that there are varying interpretations of how the *Daniel* passages fit the events, or even which events *Daniel* describes. For example, some of *Daniel*'s predictions seem to forecast events during the Roman Empire, which followed the period of Antiochus. But if they are describing Roman-period events after they happened, it should be disquieting for porphyrists were they to find copies of the book of *Daniel* at Qumran and in circulation among Jews and early Christians before the time these events occurred.

I will be the first to admit that a Babylonian-period Daniel, prophesying improbable events he will never see during his lifetime, seems unlikely. (Nah! The artsy, sissy little Greeks will never defeat the mighty Persian Empire!)[54] But if the evidence presented here is successful in showing that Daniel probably lived, and that *Daniel* probably was written, during the Babylonian exile, there is no reason not to accept the contention that (1) the prophecies were written before the events they prophesied and (2) 'Daniel' was probably Daniel. The further acceptance that God is God is a gift and, in the context of this discussion, would be mere icing on the cake.

---

[54] Their victory in the Battle of Marathon (490 BCE) was a memory no doubt overshadowed by Athens's sacking by Persia following Thermopylae in 480.

Why does it matter? It matters because a hoax scrambles up all sorts of valuable historical data. For example, the dating of *Daniel* is important for study of the living conditions of the Jews during the Babylonian exile, even though *Daniel* seems to be a source that is outside the mind-set of scholars who assiduously plead a Maccabean 'Daniel'. In their book *The Bible Unearthed*, Israel Finkelstein (b. 1949) and Neil Asher Silberman (b. 1950),[cxix] with a tacit dismissal of any possibility that 'Daniel' could have been in Babylonia during the exile, write an entire chapter, "Exile and Return (586–c. 440 BCE)", with no mention of the book of *Daniel*. With oblivious irony they say, "The Bible provides few details about the life of the exiles . . .",[cxx] whereas from 'Daniel' we have detail after detail: information about the circumstances of the young exiles, even down to their diet (1:8–16), their jobs (2:49); and of the mature and honored Daniel: his house, his library, and his prayer habits (6:10). Instead of looking to 'Daniel' for such information, they look to 'Deutero-Isaiah', where there is nothing accurate, because 'Isaiah' was not there. They look to *Ezekiel*, where they find only that "the Judahite exiles lived both in the city of Babylon and in the countryside."[cxxi]

The dating of *Daniel* is also important for the study of the historical development of theological thought. It demonstrates the development of understanding of attributes of God. If the date is wrong, all of the inferences are wrong, too. The theological significance of *Daniel* is massive. It introduces several concepts of the Messiah: it ratifies *Daniel*'s introduction of Messiah as suffering servant without hinting at a knowledge of *Isaiah* (did God give two separate prophetic messages about the suffering servant?), and it points to the life of Jesus as fulfilling the divine functions of Messianism, rather than its military and political roles.

On the popular nineteenth-century notion that theology develops according to a Hegelian pattern of thesis, antithesis, and synthesis, modern theologians say that the theology in *Daniel* is far too advanced for the sixth-century BCE, so it must have been written later—a classic example of circular reasoning. These are only a few of the insights in *Daniel* that modern theologians deny themselves and their readers, because one tends to discount any insights that seem to come from a hoax. More's the pity, since *Daniel* is not a hoax.

There are disagreements among theologians on how this plays out. For example, Thomas Krüger says that it seems indisputable that a historical-critical analysis of *Daniel* has significant consequences for its theological meaning and interpretation. I completely agree with Krüger that this analysis has these consequences. I disagree, however, about the Babylonian versus Maccabean analysis and what those theological consequences might be in the case of *Daniel*.

Krüger notes that already in the third century CE the philosopher Porphyry of Tyre realized that *Daniel* contains predictions that seem to point to events of the second century BCE with uncanny accuracy. (Why did he not note that they applied equally well if not better to events of the first century CE? Probably because he ruled out prediction *prima facie*.) Krüger assumes that therefore *Daniel*'s prophecies must be *ex eventu* predictions, which concur with the course of history until the religious crisis under Antiochus IV around the year 165 BCE, but after that date they seem to differ from the actual events. With this historical insight, Krüger says, the theological understanding of history and prophecy in *Daniel* is empirically disproved.[cxxii]

If Krüger and other modern porphyrists were correct, the book of *Daniel* would be of no theological consequence at all and would be of only antiquarian interest as a period piece of Maccabean apocalyptic literature. Its most salient features might be linguistic: its use of Hebrew and Aramaic, whereas most pseudepigraphal literature of the second century was written in Greek; and its precociously antiquarian use of the Aramaic language (note Archer's comparison with the *Genesis Apocryphon* found at Qumran). It would be unique and precocious in adopting the old style.

But it doesn't adopt the old style: it is a genuine artifact of the sixth century.

William G. Dever (b. 1933) illustrates this problem:

> In asking what the Hebrew Bible would look like if it were really a Hellenistic religious document, we need to recognize that we actually have such literature. First, there is the biblical book of Daniel, almost certainly written in the context of the Hasmonean wars of the 2nd century, although of course artificially set in the Babylonian-Persian period for literary effect, as was customary in much ancient literature. And it is no coincidence that the last chapter of Daniel clearly presupposes the Greek notion of the "immortality of the soul" totally

foreign to ancient Israel, and therefore
conspicuously absent in all the rest of
the Hebrew Bible.[cxxiii]

Here Dever demonstrates the problem of inferring the
correlation between a mistaken dating of the book and
the history and development of theological ideas. (Note
that Dever has the sensibility to qualify his dating with
the phrase "almost certainly", a nicety many porphyrists
eschew.) To what aspect(s) of the Greek notion of the
"immortality of the soul" does Dever refer? What in
Daniel differs from prior OT authors?

I suspect Dever is looking at two passages in *Daniel*
chapter 12: verses 2 and 3, which reference a resurrection, and particularly verse 5 with two personages
(angels?) by a stream, and he speaks to a man clothed in
linen. Here Dever may be reminded of the River Styx,
where Greek mythology has those who die ferried
across to Hades by the boatman Charon. But *Daniel* has
no ferry or boatman, no frogs (as in Aristophanes' eponymous play, about questions of life after death), no
mention of anyone going across. In fact, *Daniel*'s man
clothed in linen points *up*ward with both hands, whereas in Greek mythology, the god of the dead is the god
of the *under*world. The river symbolism seems to have
no Hellenistic significance here. But because he and
others put the date of *Daniel* in the second century,
Dever assumes that the idea of immortality of the soul
was absent from Jewish theology until the second
century, where it was introduced by a Hellenistic-period
'Daniel'.

But even if *Daniel* were Hellenistic, would 'Daniel' depend upon a "Greek notion of the 'immortality of the soul' totally foreign to ancient Israel"? Or does the book in any case articulate a Jewish theology of immortality that predates the Greek by centuries if not millennia? I argue for the latter.

There are two notable aspects of afterlife in *Daniel*: (1) the immortality of the soul in a conscious afterlife, and (2) the reward or punishment of the soul, based on the mortal life and deeds of the person. In chapter 12 'Daniel' (ca. 620–ca. 530?) illustrates both:

> 2 Many who sleep in the dust of the earth
> shall awake, some to everlasting life, and
> some to shame and everlasting contempt.
> 3 And those who are wise will be like the
> brightness of the firmament; and those who
> turn many to righteousness, shall shine like
> the stars forever.

Daniel does not dwell on the afterlife. We see below much more in the OT elsewhere.

There are also two aspects of the Greek afterlife. (1) the need for proper burial to free the soul from its earthly bonds. The alternatives seem to have been either unhappy wandering or a peaceful rest. The second depends on the first. In the burial rite the Greek view seems to be both more ritualistic than the Hebrew and, at the same time, more simplistic in purpose: (2) to allow the spirit of the departed to find rest.[55] Aristopha-

---

55 The reader will of course note that both analyses are necessarily oversimplifications. That does not destroy the comparison.

nes (446-386 BCE) seems to illustrate a later development in *The Frogs*, where the departed seem to have more wisdom than the living, and also have a possibility of coming back to earth (although one wonders to what end).

At the time of dramatist Euripides (480–406 BCE), Greek ideas about proper burial observances seem to include the notion that the dead person enters a state of rest not available until a ritual burial of the body is performed.[56] Think of Antigone's anxiety to bury her brother Orestes in Euripides' play *Orestes*. The three plays, *Agamemnon* by Aeschylus (525–456 BCE), *Elektra* by Sophocles (497–406 BCE), and *Orestes* by Euripides, illustrate the ritualistic aspect of this Greek concept of afterlife. In Greek drama, from the reeds along the River Styx comes the mocking chorus of Aristophanes' play, *The Frogs* (405 BCE), a comedy about who is to stay in Hades.[cxxiv] Another example of Greek dramatic thinking is found in *Agamemnon*, where Aeschylus has the chorus sing,

> Ah! What is mortal life? When prosperous.
> A shadow can o'erturn it, and, when fallen,
> A swipe of the wet sponge blurs the picture
> out... Who but a god goes woundless all the
> way?

Here it is not the virtuous life that goes woundless, deserving eternal bliss, nor the perfidious life that is blurred by the swipe of a sponge. Mortality is fickle; its first priority is proper burial.

---

[56] *Prosthesis* (viewing), *ekphora* (procession), interment.

The Hebrew Scriptures, on the other hand, assume that the soul is immortal but require no burial strictures. It is evident in the Scriptures long before a sixth-century 'Daniel' or fifth-century Greek drama. There are several OT counterexamples. *Genesis* may reflect a tradition a thousand years earlier than the epics of Homer.

Genesis 37:26–36 (ca. eighteenth century BCE?): Here the young Joseph's brothers give their father, Jacob, Joseph's bloodied coat of many colors to deceive him into thinking that Joseph is dead. Jacob responds, "I shall mourn for him until I go down to Sheol where I shall see my son." Jacob assumed that they would meet in the sweet bye and bye, and he intended to mourn for him until that time came. He assumed that his son Joseph did not vanish with his body's death, nor that his shade would wander the earth for want of a proper burial. He implies that he himself would die someday, but that his postmortem self would be cognizant of meeting Joseph after death. Is this simply an unconscious rest, a sleep? If he says, "I shall see my son," I think not.

Genesis 49:33: Here the aged Jacob was dying in Egypt. He instructed his sons to take his bones from Egypt back to the cave at Machpelah, where his grandparents, parents, and wife were buried. He and his sons knew that it would be months if not years before they could go back to this burial ground. But meeting his loved ones in Sheol was to be accomplished immediately after death: "he drew up his feet into the bed, breathed his last, and was gathered unto his people." This demonstrates the Hebrew disregard for burial rites in order for the dead to find peace. Jacob had no plans to roam the earth as a shade until his bones could be buried, as the Greek tradition would become.

At *1 Samuel* 28 (ca. tenth century BCE), the prophet Samuel had died and was buried at Ramah. King Saul was about to go to battle with the Philistines and called on the Lord, but the Lord did not answer him. So Saul consulted the witch of Endor, who brought up the prophet Samuel (presumably from Sheol), and Samuel said, "Why have you disturbed me by bringing me up?", so we can infer that his afterlife, like that of the Greeks, was calm and undisturbed (and that it was down, not up, as the figure in *Daniel* implies). In verses 15–19 the Lord sent Samuel back from the dead to deliver a message to Saul, namely that Saul and his sons would be with him (i.e., dead) the next day. Their bodies were not buried the next day, although this passage implies that their souls joined Samuel in death. In both the case of Jacob and that of Saul, it was the person (soul?) who went to Sheol, a place of reunion and of rest, while in both cases the bodies remained unburied.

Moving a thousand years from the age of the Patriarchs to the classic prophetic period of the divided monarchy, we find in *Isaiah* (ca. 760–673 BCE) at 14:9 an oracle concerning Babylon, which will be destroyed. The people of Israel are told to taunt the king of Babylon, who will "find Sheol beneath, stirred up to meet him when he comes". At *Isaiah* 14:10 the shades of his fellow kings greet the king of Babylon: he had been proud, strong, and haughty, but "you are now become as weak as we." *Isaiah* 14:18–20: "You are cast out of the grave (*qeber*) like a pruned branch, ... you shall not be joined with them in burial." This seems to introduce an element of punishment and reward. Here Sheol is where the evil and mighty are brought low, to everlasting shame and contempt.

I timidly suggest that there is a development here from simple but cognizant immortality to postmortem punishment and reward in which Jewish theology far outpaces Greek philosophy in subtlety as it is represented in drama. Few scholars date any part of *Isaiah* later than the reconstruction of Jerusalem (fifth century), and this particular section is generally thought to be *Primo-Isaiah*, written by Isaiah of Jerusalem, eighth century BCE. This not only antedates 'Daniel', whether early or late, but it also antedates the Greek tragedians. The Greek poet Homer, author of the *Iliad* and the *Odyssey*, and the Hebrew prophet Isaiah of Jerusalem were probably roughly contemporary.

Dever implies that 'Daniel' acquired the idea of immortality of the soul from the Greeks. Note that Dever is not claiming that the Greek notion of afterlife, a notion he says comes so late to Judaism, is a fully developed resurrection life, which seems to be primarily a product of the New Testament. It seems strange, then, for Dever to say that the soul's continuity after the death of the body was a concept absent from Jewish theology. It is true that with 'Daniel' there is a more developed understanding of postmortem punishment and reward and perhaps the initial theology of the postmortem awareness of the presence of God. But there is every reason to assume that it is not borrowed from the Greeks.

Dever is an expert on archaeological *realia*. He knows pottery shapes, perhaps surpassing all others in this field. But I suspect that his interest and study have not focused on the development of theological thought. So I submit that Dever not only misplaces the time period within which 'Daniel' wrote, but also fails to notice the older traces of the soul's assumed postmortem existence in the Bible.

The first time I visited the Megiddo archaeological site I jumped to a conclusion about architecture similar to Dever's conclusion about the immortality of the soul. Looking at a proto-Aeolian capital from one of the pillars there, I thought, "Hmmm. It looks like a crude attempt at copying a Greek Ionic capital with scrolls at the corners." Later I compared the dates of the two architectural styles. Megiddo dates from 7000 to 586 BCE (after which the site was unoccupied). Ionic columns date from the fifth century BCE—that is, 400s. Silly me. Maybe in each case the Greeks got the idea from the Jews—the afterlife and the columns—instead of the other way round (although I have no idea how). With the architecture, the Greeks developed the column to a high degree of aesthetic beauty. With the soul's continuity and the theology of immortality the Jews win hands down.

The experts seem to find it just as difficult to decide which ancient writers to trust about historical facts.

In 1936 D. S. Rice discovered in the ruins of the Great Mosque in Harran two stelae of Nabonidus, used there secondarily as paving stones. Both are in typical ...

...stela[57] form, ending in a semicircle which contains in bas relief the figure of the king in adoration before the symbols of the Sun, Ishtar, and the Moon. The lower part of each monolith contains the inscription in three columns of about 50 lines.[cxxv]

The Darius-the-Mede question may have been answered by one of the Harran stelae, in which King Nabonidus of Babylon gives an account of the events of his reign.[cxxvi] In 546 BCE Nabonidus here refers to *the kings of Egypt, of the Medes, and of the Arabs.* The "king of the Medes" mentioned in the stele at that time was Cyrus II (the Great), by then king of the Persians, the Medes, and the Lydians. Cyrus would later unseat Nabonidus to become king of the Babylonians as well. Was Cyrus the Great a Mede as well as a Persian? Well, yes. He was king of the Median Empire. Was he also called Darius? Possibly. Probably. Here we have title linkage, but not yet name linkage.

Yet another issue arises in relation to *Daniel*'s popularity at Qumran. If the experts were right about *Daniel* being a Maccabean-period hoax, it is amazing that any copy or fragment at all has been found that dates from the period in which the experts say it was written. A Maccabean-period *Daniel* should now be of no theological or historical importance, as many experts attest. Some scholars go so far as to argue that the LXX Greek translation of *Daniel* as a whole preceded the Hebrew Proto-Masoretic version.[cxxvii] But eight Hebrew-Ara-

---

[57] Singuar 'stele' ("steelee"): An upright slab or a pillar with an inscription.

maic-language *Daniel* copies at Qumran make this improbable.

Emanuel Tov (b. 1941) notes that it remains puzzling why the two sources—the LXX and the Hebrew—are so divergent in chapters 3–6 and not in the remainder of the book. He suggests that these chapters may have circulated separately.[cxxviii] Even the often-proposed 165 BCE date of writing the autograph seems improbable if one tries to account for all of this copying and circulating occurring in the short period allotted by a Maccabean (167–160 BCE) date of writing. The rewritings and translatings and circulatings separately to which Tov alludes do not mean that Tov himself has espoused an early dating of *Daniel*. Heaven forfend! I merely note that from Tov's analysis of what he calls this "strange book", it is hard to see how a Maccabean dating might fit.

The popularity of *Daniel* at Qumran brings up an interesting side issue: were the Dead Sea Scrolls actually at Qumran in the first century, or should they properly be dated to the medieval period? Is there a more general hoax than *Daniel* involved? There must be! So argued Solomon Zeitlin (1908–1976), a scholar who specialized in the history of the Jewish Second Commonwealth or Second Temple Period. Zeitlin's study of this period illumi-nated our understanding of the Jewish canonical pro-cess (ch. 4, above). He wrote voluminously of that per-iod but was completely skeptical of the Dead Sea arch-aeological findings, based on philological issues he found with the first publication of photographic images of the scrolls.

Zeitlin's first concern is the War Scroll: the "War Between the Sons of Light and the Sons of Darkness". He notes that the sons, Aram, Uz, Hul, Togar, and Masa were no longer mentioned during the Second Commonwealth:

> We note that he also mentioned Togar. In the Pentateuch we have Togarmah... In the late rabbinic literature Togaramah referred to Turkey. The name Togar was employed for a Turk and came into vogue in the late Hebrew literature, and never occurred earlier. We cannot explain how the word Togar appeared in the Scroll unless we assume that it was composed in a very late period. This assumption is strengthened by the fact that parentheses as well as connecting lines between two words are used in this Scroll.[cxxix]

Zeitlin found spellings in the *Isaiah* Scroll to be "on a par with the spelling in many writings of the Middle Ages", indicating that it was written by an uneducated Jew.

> No Jew in the Second Commonwealth could have written the scrolls. At that time only those who knew Hebrew wrote, but those who did not, did not write. Not only are words missing in the text, but phrases and full verses.[cxxx]

Zeitlin notes that *matres lectiones* were used in the scrolls, a spelling technique that used some of the letters (all consonants) to indicate vowel sounds that Zeitlin insists were unknown in the Scriptures until they were invented by Rabbi Akiva (50–137 CE). Zeitlin gives example after example of instances where the Dead Sea Scrolls exhibit spellings, word usages, correction tech-niques, and other practices that had not been found in the literature until the medieval period.

So Zeitlin suspected a hoax. Zeitlin's list of suspicions begins with the "discovery" of the scrolls. He enumerates the divergent accounts.

- The apparently earliest account proffered about the finding of the scrolls involves Bedouin traders (not shepherds) who were taking goods from Jordan to Bethlehem by way of the Dead Sea in the spring of 1947. They saw caves with scrolls protruding from jars, took the scrolls (and jars?) to a sheik in Bethlehem, who sent them to Syrian Christians, who sent them to their metropolitan at St. Mark's Orthodox Convent in Jerusalem.
- Archbishop Samuel's account involves two merchants, and five scrolls in a bag, all of which he bought from merchants in the summer of 1947. He contacted the president of Hebrew University, who sent scholars to see them, with no result.
- A third account, by Professor E. Sukenik, tells of learning of the scrolls from a Muslim antiquarian from Bethlehem in November 1947. He bought two jars and some fragments from the merchant.
- The earliest account of a visit to the site by archaeologists was G.L. Harding and Roland de Vaux, who found nothing except cigarette stubs, a Roman lamp, and a cooking pot.

o   In the February 1954 *Biblical Archaeologist* Frank
    Moore Cross wrote what became the standard
    popular account:

> One spring day in 1947 a shepherd,
> Muhammad Dib, roamed looking
> for a lost sheep. He sat down and
> threw stones at a hole in the rocky
> cliff opposite him. One went into
> the hole and made a sound of some-
> thing shattering. He fled, but later
> came back with friends, climbed in-
> to the hole, found broken pottery
> and leather scrolls, and the rest is
> history.[cxxxi]

No archaeologist saw those first scrolls *in situ*. They
were purchased from merchants who sold antiquities.
Zeitlin seems to have suspected that the Bedouin and
the antiquities merchants were in cahoots with one another, and pawned off scrolls from the Hebron Jewish
community's collection of medieval scrolls as archaeological finds. His suspicions were based on his scholarly familiarity with the Jewish literature and religious
practice of the Second Commonwealth through the
medieval and modern periods.

Zeitlin had voluminous paleographical evidence. Was
he right?

No. He seems to be mistaken about the *Isaiah* Scroll
and all of the others now catalogued. He may have been
right about some hoaxmanship surrounding one manuscript that seems to have quietly vanished: a medieval
Haftorah (lectionary) scroll that is referred to in the
group of five scrolls first offered to Samuel and never

again. A hoaxer may have tried to sneak a medieval scroll in with some genuine ancient scrolls, and later thought better of even trying. Of the five scrolls offered, the fifth seems to have disappeared without a ripple.

These have now been submitted to radiocarbon dating and found to date from the period between the second century BCE and the 68 CE. A paper published in 1992 tested fourteen scrolls from the Dead Sea area. To calibrate the technique, four papyri were tested that had internal dates: these were samples from the caves at

- Wadi Daliyeh (354–351 BCE)
- Wadi Seyel (130–131 CE)
- Maraba'at (134 CE)
- Kirbet Mird (744 CE)

The other ten scrolls were then tested and found to date within the period when the Dead Sea community at Qumran and other nearby archaeological sites were thought to have been active:

- The *Isaiah* parchment (125–100 BCE)
- The book of *Samuel* parchment (100–75 BCE)
- The *Genesis Apocryphon* (end of 1st c. BCE)[cxxxii]

This changes the playing field. The team performing the radiocarbon dating was meticulous. The technique on organic materials of this period has become quite precise. So much for Professor Zeitlin's cries of hoax and his suspicions that the findings from Qumran dated from the tenth rather than the first century. What does this mean?

What it does not mean is that Zeitlin was a careless scholar, or that the issues that aroused his concern about a hoax were mistaken. As far as the evidence available without the Dead Sea Scrolls themselves, Zeitlin was right as rain. But given additional radio-carbon dating, it also means that the ground has shifted under Zeitlin's data. It means that an authentically ancient *Isaiah* scroll could exhibit paleographical characteristics of an inferior medieval text. It means that Rabbi Akiva did not invent the *matres lectiones* after all.

I don't know whether Professor Zeitlin ever was able to make the paradigm shift in his thinking to incorporate the new Dead Sea information about the Second Jewish Commonwealth. It takes a lot of humility and openness to make such a shift in one's thinking about a field of study one has pursued all one's life.

We can take away from Zeitlin's contretemps several lessons. The first is that of crass monetary market value. The *Isaiah* scroll on the marketplace today would bring millions, if it is from the first or second century BCE. If it were a tenth-century scroll, it would be worth somewhere in the range of $10,000–$20,000 on the open market. To have downgraded the Dead Sea Scrolls accurately to medieval artifacts would have been financially devastating for those who had already raised millions of shekels for the Shrine of the Book, a museum —at that time only prospective—for the display and explanation of these ancient artifacts. Thank goodness it is authentic.

The second lesson we can use is the relative precision and objective verifiability of carbon dating that allows us to calibrate the philology on which Zeitlin was relying. It means that the types of copy errors that Zeitlin disparaged in the *Isaiah* scroll were made in the first and second centuries BCE as well as in the tenth CE. It means that the words Zeitlin assured us were not in use until the medieval period were indeed in use ten centuries earlier.

Within the brotherhood of *Daniel* scholars, Professor Zeitlin gives us another valuable lesson. When must we assume that "all the best scholars" are right? In spite of his encyclopedic knowledge of the Second Temple period, Zeitlin seems to have bet the wrong way more than once. In his 1933 monograph on the OT canon, there is no mention of a *Daniel* pseudepigraphy. Here he explains, for example, why Ben Sira is not canonical:

> [T]he rabbis were of the opinion that prophecy ceased from Israel after Daniel in the Persian period [for which he cites Seder Olam Rabba, XXX].[58] Therefore all the books written after that time cannot be considered a part of the Holy Scriptures. The book of Ben Sira was written in the Hellenistic period and that was the reason for its exclusion from the canon.[cxxxiii]

Throughout this 1933 monograph, Zeitlin gives no hint of questioning that *Daniel* might be from the Maccabean period. Here, in an offhand aside, *Daniel* is accepted as being from the Persian period. And not only *Daniel*, but its prophecy, leaving no room for two authors, with the *ex eventu* prophecies in the second century and the rest of the book (if there is such) in the sixth.

---

[58] For which he cites Seder Olam Rabba, XXX.

By 1962, however, Zeitlin has changed his tune about *Daniel*:

> Whether or not the book of Daniel is a compilation of one or two authors, its last chapters were undoubtedly written after the purification of the Temple by Judah Makkabee.[cxxxiv]

And again, "Chapters 7–12 of Daniel were written after 165 BCE."[cxxxv] Yet despite its presumed Maccabean origin, to which he seems to have gravitated by 1962, Zeitlin saw no conflict in the canonization of *Daniel* with the Prophets before the conclave in 65 CE and later in the Writings, which he says were initially made holy in 65.[cxxxvi] This, in contrast to his 1933 standard that prophecy ceased with the Persian *Daniel*. He cannot object that the prophetic *Daniel* was the early Persian one: it is precisely the *ex eventu* prophecy that he is claiming to be Maccabean. So what happened? Where is the scholarly consistency?

Although Zeitlin was a painstaking scholar, he has come up with the wrong conclusions at least twice. If he was right in 1933 in holding that *Daniel*'s predictive prophecies were written in the Persian period, then he was wrong in 1962 in proclaiming that they were from the Maccabean period. And if he was right about a Macca-bean faux 'Daniel', he was wrong about the ancient rabbis being of the opinion that prophecy ceased with a Persian *Daniel*. With his claim that the Dead Sea Scrolls are medieval, he is again wrong. His paleography and philology are no match for radiocarbon dating when it comes to organic materials several hundred or more years old. As to which other time he was wrong, I leave it for the reader to speculate.

9
Josephus and Alexander

Josephus (37 – 100 CE) seems to prove that the book of *Daniel* was in the Temple in Jerusalem, and that Alexander the Great (356–323 BCE) saw it when he visited the Temple. So my early dating of *Daniel* is a slam-dunk.

But porphyrists say Josephus must be wrong. Of course if they are right in saying that *Daniel* was not written until the second century, it could not possibly be in the Temple in the late fourth century. So we need to look into Josephus' competence as a historian.

Joseph ben Mattathias, later known as Titus Flavius Josephus, was born in Jerusalem to a priestly family distantly connected to the Hasmonean royal line.[59] As a young man at the time when Israel rebelled against Roman rule, he was in charge of the defense of the Galilean town of Jotapata, which was besieged and defeated by the Roman general Vespasian and his son Titus. (Both later became Caesars.)

Josephus became a captive of the Romans and provided them with information about Israel that may have facilitated the Roman quashing of the Jewish rebellion, an inevitable defeat in any case. He went to Rome and lived out his life there in relative tranquility, writing several works that survive. In *The Antiquities of the Jews*

---

[59] That is, to the Maccabees or Hasmoneans, not the Davidic royal line.

Josephus tells us that a few generations after the Jews were allowed to return from captivity in Babylonia, the priests of the Temple in Jerusalem showed Alexander the Great a copy of the book of *Daniel* (ca. 332 BCE). If Josephus is accurate, this is a piece of evidence that puts *Daniel* quite squarely in history 150 years before the hoax was supposed to have occurred.

But a preponderance of scholars—the dean's ninety-seven percent—say that Josephus cannot be accurate here, because *Daniel* had not been written at the time of Alexander, so they say. So therefore Josephus must be wrong. (Circular reasoning) Momigliano is adamant:

> Alexander never went to Jerusalem.[cxxxvii]

He gives no particular reasons or evidence. He is expansive, however. Reading Momigliano is somewhat like watching someone skipping stones across a pond. It requires skill to do it as well as he does. His next several stones go like this:

> But Jewish legends which found their way
> into the Alexander romance fondly narra-
> ted the encounter between the High Priest
> and the new King of Kings. ... The memory
> of Alexander remained one of those pieces
> of folklore the Jews could share with their
> neighbors.[cxxxviii]

Is there something strange about this argument? It isn't an argument, presents no evidence, and offers nothing but bombast. Yet it and its variations have found wide acceptance in the academic community.

About Josephus, Elliot Binns says,

> When Alexander visited the Temple (Ant.
> IX, viii, 3) he inspected the book [of Dani-
> el]. But as *the whole account of the visit is proba-
> bly an invention*, his testimony is not of much
> value.[cxxxix] (emphasis added)

Why does Binns label Josephus' account as an invention? He doesn't say, nor do John J. Collins and the
many others since Driver. The view seems to be so
widely held that no one feels any need to justify it. But
let's look into unjustifying it.

Alexander the Great was notoriously religious. As was
fashionable, he considered himself to be descended
from heroes—in his case, Perseus and Heracles—and
from the gods Zeus and Ammon, whom he revered.[cxl]
After his victory in the battle at Issus, the cities of the
eastern Mediterranean, which were paying tribute to
Persia, welcomed him as a liberator—all but Tyre and
Gaza. Tyre accepted him, but the Tyrians refused to let
him enter the temple of their god Ammon to worship.[60]
Alexander insisted on his terms, which included wor-
shipping at the temple of any city he conquered, but
especially the worship of Ammon, his supposed ancestor. So he besieged Tyre and finally won, but only after
building a causeway from the mainland to the island
city.

Another instance of his preoccupation with temples
and gods occurred after his (peaceful) conquest of

---

[60] For the myth describing his relation to Ammon, see *The Romance of
Alexander the Great*, by Pseudo-Callisthenes, third century CE.

Egypt. While there, he insisted on paying a visit to an oracle of Ammon situated at an oasis deep into the Libyan desert at Siwah. On the way to the coast from Memphis, he designated a location and laid out the city of Alexandria, which his engineers afterward completed. He traveled along the coast for more than two hundred kilometers and then headed into the trackless desert toward Siwah, according to his biographer Arrian.[61] The distance from Alexandria to Siwah is 841 kilometers (522 miles).[62] So Alexander insisted on going more than a thousand miles out of his way to worship Ammon and consult the oracle, with no military or mercantile objective. This is a long, hard day's drive on interstates at 70 mph. He and his retinue nearly died of thirst in the desert. At Siwah he paid obeisance to the god Ammon and consulted the oracle. Then he retraced his journey to Memphis and to Tyre to complete the administrative initiation of making Tyre his own Hellenized city.

Kasher suggests another reason that Alexander was occupied, if not preoccupied, with temples:

> It should be recalled that sacrificing in
> a temple was considered by Alexander
> a ceremonial act intended to exhibit a
> change in political reality, an amend-
> ment that entailed the population's re-
> cognition of his authority as the new
> ruler. Furthermore, performing such

---

[61] Arrian is one of the more dependable extant Alexander biographers, but nevertheless he wrote nearly four hundred years after Alexander's death.
[62] This distance may be as the plane flies, in which case he would have traveled even farther.

an action should be evaluated on one hand
as an attempt to placate the local god, and
on the other to conciliate the population...
Alexander's ceremonial presence in the temple was thus tantamount to 'divine recogni-
tion' and understood as such by the subject
peoples.[cxli]

A trip to the Temple in Jerusalem would fit this protocol well: He would be saying, in effect, I am your new
ruler. You will honor me as such, and pay your tribute
to me (rather than to Persia) from now on.

Given his predilection for worshiping the gods of the
peoples he conquered, it is no surprise that he would
want to visit the Temple in Jerusalem. A diagram (below) will show that a seemingly purposeless visit to Siwah in the Libyan desert dwarfs any difficulty of making a side trip to Jerusalem. The Jewish capital is by
comparison almost a suburb of Tyre or Gaza, each of
which he besieged for boring months on end. The Siwah visit, though, does not fit this profile but instead a
case of sheer obsession with temples and oracles. Compared to the 841 kilometers to Siwah and another 841
back, a visit to Jerusalem from Gaza or Tyre would
have been a mere afternoon stroll. Alexander might
have chosen to make the 82.9-kilometer (51-mile) trip
from Gaza to Jerusalem or the 165-kilometer (102-mile)
trip from Tyre to Jerusalem during either siege, just to
relieve the tedium.

Binns says that Josephus' whole account of the visit to
Jerusalem is probably an invention.[cxlii] But need we, too,
assume that it was?

According to Josephus, Alexander made his trip to Jerusalem after his conquest of Gaza and before going to Egypt, just to visit the temple there and perhaps with no other purpose. But we also have two other occasions to place him in close proximity to Jerusalem for administrative and economic reasons not related to his proclivity for religion. Hence we can probably put Alexander into the Palestinian hinterland on three occasions, at three sites: at the Temple, at a balsam plantation, and in Samaria.

A. B. Bosworth, writing about the methods of ancient historians in general, and Alexander's biographers in particular, says that

> when writing up a period already blessed with historical narratives, ancient writers did not add bogus "facts" out of their imagination. The nature of the game was to operate with the material at one's disposal, identifying and criticizing falsehood and bias, combining details from several sources into a composite picture not paralleled in any single source, but not adding invention of one's own... I am not suggesting that "secondary" historians were copyists. Selection was a part of the creative process. When faced with a multiplicity of sources, a historian would opt for the treatment most conducive to exemplary moralizing, and the same episode could be shaped to convey very different messages.[cxliii]

Many scholars consider Josephus unreliable, some perhaps *because* he places the book of *Daniel* in the Temple to be shown to Alexander the Great. Kasher may not be included in this category: he says that although some legendary motifs found their way into Josephus' story, this is not a reason to discredit the story in its entirety. He points out that Arrian, Curtius Rufus, Plutarch, Diodorus, and others integrated legendary motifs in writing about Alexander.[cxliv] If Alexander (or any other subject) regards a phenomenon as an omen (e.g., birds or snakes guiding them to the Siwah oasis) and acts on it, historians would be unfaithful to their calling not to include it in their accounts. What Kasher and others regard as legendary motifs (e.g., prophetic dreams, oracles, and prophetic writing) both their sources and their subject—Alexander—regarded as modus operandi: "This is the way one makes decisions." Only by including them would they be accurate as historians. Historians should distinguish between real influences on their subjects, such as oracles, and what the historians regard as apocryphal, such as George Washington and the cherry tree—legendary stories that may have developed after the fact. Sometimes historians fail because their mind-set discounts or ignores some of the evidence of dreams and oracles that not only shaped historical actions but in their doing so became part of the event, as we have here with Alexander and *Daniel*. This is true of both ancient and modern historians: what is included in their accounts depends on what they themselves consider to be important.

Josephus' is the only extant account that places Alexander the Great in Jerusalem, and it is almost universally discredited by modern porphyrists. Several reasons are given why this story should not be taken at face value:

- o Josephus tells of prophetic dreams, so anything he says can be drummed out of court. (Fallaciously: here they use an understood disqualified premise; "Accounts of prophetic dreams must be historically fictitious, so any account of events that include them cannot be historical.")
- o There is no corroborative evidence from other writers on Alexander; therefore it didn't happen. (A fallacious argument from silence that is discussed below in this context.)
- o Josephus reports that Alexander was shown the *Daniel* scroll a century and a half before modern academics think it was written. (Here they commit the fallacy of begging the question: whether or not the book already had been written is precisely the question at issue here.)

Is Josephus a careless historian? I am sometimes amazed at the superciliousness of our era. We seem to assume that the ancients were idiots, whereas if we ourselves were not so blockheaded we would be able to glean a great deal of useful data from them. Our scholars often find that ancient writers know more about their own times than our historians do, yet we nevertheless refuse to learn anything from Josephus that is not confirmed elsewhere. Often we assume that the other ancient sources we have were earlier and closer to Alexander than was Josephus. But this assumption is mistaken.

The surviving Alexander evidence is in works written by the following authors, in chronological order:
- o Diodorus of Sicily (probably active 60–30 BCE)
- o Curtius Rufus (active 41–54 CE)
- o Pliny the Elder (23–79 CE)

- ○ Josephus (37–100 CE)
- ○ Plutarch (46–120 CE)
- ○ Arrian (ca. 86–160 CE)
- ○ Justin (third century CE)
- ○ Pseudo-Callisthenes (third century CE)

We notice that Diodorus, the earliest, nevertheless lived at least two centuries after Alexander and the events he writes about. The first six writers here should be classified as secondary sources at best. Justin is at least tertiary, and Pseudo-Callisthenes is writing a romance. Where did they get their information? From primary sources, now lost, the most prominent being the real Callisthenes, Alexander's official chronicler. Some of Alexander's officers and soldiers also made both written and oral accounts, also lost.

In spite of the modern scholars who maintain that there is no moment in Alexander's busy schedule when he could have had time to go to Jerusalem, we have evidence that he was either there or very close on three occasions. In them we note that we can go far in corroborating Josephus' craft as a historian.

Let's consider his account of the Samaritan leader Sanballat, which is confirmed by irrefutable external evidence. Until the 1960s the dean's ninety-seven percent claimed that Josephus was confused about Sanballat. The Bible says quite clearly that Sanballat of Samaria lived at the time of Ezra and Nehemiah (Neh. 2:19; 4:1, 7; 6:1). So if Josephus puts Sanballat several generations later, Josephus doesn't know what he is writing about. So they say.

The gist of Josephus' account is this: Both Samaria and Judea had sworn fealty to Darius III of Persia, and Alexander defeated Darius' overwhelming forces at the Battle of Issus (333 BCE). Alexander sent word to both Samaria and Judea asking for support. Darius had lost his family and much of his army at Issus, but not his ego, and he was preparing to fight again. Noticing which way the wind seemed to be blowing, the Samaritan ruler, Sanballat, switched sides and gave Alexander seven thousand men for the siege of Tyre. Alexander sent a letter to the Jewish high priest telling him that whatever he had formerly paid Darius in tribute, he now should pay to Alexander. The high priest replied that he had given his oath to Darius and would honor that oath as long as Darius was alive.[63] Alexander was furious. So when Alexander approached Jerusalem, the inhabitants had every reason to fear complete destructtion of their city and slavery for its citizens. But that did not happen. As Josephus tells it, Alexander went to Jerusalem sometime, perhaps during the sieges of the seacoast ports of Tyre and Gaza, and either before or after he conquered Egypt, or both--probably before, because Josephus says, "Now Alexander, when he had taken Gaza, made haste to go up to Jerusalem." Jerusalem was an easy one-day ride from Gaza.

Th Lord had warned the high priest in a dream not to resist but with the other priests in full ceremonial dress to greet Alexander and usher him into the city, which

---

[63] This Darius is not to be confused with Darius the Mede, who ruled Babylonia as a tribute state of the Persian Empire under Cyrus the Great. Perhaps he was Cyrus the Great. That was in the middle of the sixth century; this is toward the end of the fourth.

they did. Alexander went forward and knelt before the high priest, explaining afterward that it was not to the priest that he gave obeisance, but to the priest's God. He also explained that back in Macedonia he had had a dream in which he saw these very men in these strange costumes. So Josephus:

> And he came into the city and when he went up into the Temple, he offered sacrifice to God, according to the high priest's direction, and magnificently treated both the high priest and the priests. *And when the book of Daniel was shown to him, wherein Daniel declared that one of the Greeks would destroy the empire of the Persians he supposed that he himself was the person intended; and as he was then glad,* he dismissed the multitude for the present, but the next day he called them to him, and bade them ask what favors they pleased of him: whereupon the high priest desired that they might enjoy the laws of their forefathers, and might pay no tribute on the seventh year. He granted all they desired; and when they entreated him that he would permit the Jews in Babylon and Media to enjoy their own laws also, he willingly promised to do hereafter what they desired.[cxlv] (emphasis added)

The *Daniel* passage that was shown to Alexander[64] was probably 8:2–7:

> 2 I was in Shushan (Susa) by the Ulai canal.
> 3 I looked up: and as I watched, there in

---

[64] It would have been read to him translated into Greek from the Hebrew and Aramaic, because the translation into Greek the Septuagint—was still more than a century into the future.

front of the stream stood a ram with two horns. The horns were long, but one was longer than the other, and the longer one came up later [than the other]. ⁴ I saw the ram pushing to the west, north and south; and no animals could stand up against it; nor was there anyone that could rescue from its power. ⁵ So it did as it pleased and became very strong. I was beginning to understand, when a male goat came from the west, passing over the whole earth without touching the ground. The goat had a prominent horn between its eyes. ⁶ It approached the ram with the two horns, which I had seen standing in front of the river and charged it with savage force. ⁷ I watched as it advanced on the ram, filled with rage against it, and struck the ram, breaking its two horns. The ram was powerless to stand against it. It threw the ram to the ground and trampled it down, and there was no one that could rescue it from the goat's power.

A few verses later (20–21), the angel Gabriel is sent by someone off stage to explain the vision—to give the key to this *roman à clef*:

²⁰ You saw a ram with two horns which are the kings of Media and Persia. ²¹ The shaggy male goat is the king of Greece, and the prominent horn between its eyes is the first king. [65]

So it is easy to see why Alexander would be encouraged by this predictive prophecy to advance to Susa, firm in

[65] This translation is from the Hebrew/Aramaic *Daniel*, not the LXX, which was heavily glossed with additions by its well-meaning but misleading translator.

his conviction that he would be victorious over Darius'
Medo-Persian army. And he was.

Here we have two levels of evidence. We have what
Josephus is aware of telling us: namely, that
- o   Alexander came to Jerusalem,
- o   visited the Temple,
- o   and was shown the *Daniel* scroll by the priests.

This may be true, or it may not be. Binns and others
claim that it is not. But whether or not this is true,
Josephus thought that it was. He got it from what he
thought was good authority. He was not restricted by
the assumption that predictive prophecy and other
miracles are hoaxes.

We have also what Josephus is unaware that he is telling
us—what he and other Jewish scholars believed about
Daniel in the first century CE:
- o   Josephus had no reason to think that he was
      providing evidence in a future controversy about
      when 'Daniel' wrote.
- o   There was no discussion of false authorship of the
      Daniel scroll.
- o   The historical Daniel was thought to be who and
      what the book of *Daniel* says he was.
- o   There seems to have been no rumor that the book
      was recent to the first century historian, Josephus.
- o   It was uncontroversial that *Daniel* declared that a
      Greek would destroy the Medo-Persian Empire.
- o   The Greeks were named as such at 8:20–21, and this
      was not thought to be interpolated.
- o   After Alexander-the-he-goat (at 8:21 'Daniel' calls
      the king of Greece a shaggy male goat) was dead, a
      fourth kingdom would destroy the Greek Empire.

- ○ Josephus knew that the empire that destroyed the Greek kingdoms was the Roman. (Josephus wrote during the Roman Empire.)
- ○ The Temple priests were expecting Alexander's victorious empire, from the prophecies in the book of *Daniel*. They had read the book and now they were watching the movie being filmed on site, with themselves in minor roles. They knew the plot as it was unfolding before them.
- ○ At the time of Josephus, all this was commonplace knowledge (even perhaps widespread) in Judea and Rome. It was not contested. The multiple copies of *Daniel* at Qumran attest to this.

If Josephus' account is accurate on all points, both conscious and unconscious, it is evidence that *Daniel* was not only already written, but that the scroll was in the Temple and was respected by the Temple priests, a century and a half before the book is generally considered to have been written (332 vs. 164 BCE). It probably was not yet canonical; only the Torah was holy writ. The prophets were not yet canonized, and *Daniel* with them, until sometime later. The only basis for the modern porphyrist contention that Alexander the Great never went to Jerusalem is an argument from silence: "We don't have another account corroborating it, therefore it didn't happen."

Silence is one of those wobbly argument forms that depend for their validity entirely on their context. ("It is not mentioned in the extant literature, therefore it did not happen.") Sometimes the inference is justified and other times not. For example, "Williams didn't score."

If you get a text message from an impeccable source—
your best friend—who was at the game, and he texted[66]
you every play in the game—exactly who made every
point—and he didn't mention Williams, then it is probably safe to conclude that Williams didn't score. On
the other hand, look at "Jones didn't score." If the account of that game was an old letter from somebody's
grandfather about a game played before you were born,
and you don't know whether the writer tells about all
the goals, and he doesn't mention Jones, it is not safe to
say that just because he wasn't mentioned Jones didn't
score. He may have, in this case. And it appears that the
evidence for Alexander's campaign is more like Jones
game than Williams.

So what kind of a historian is Josephus? Did he invent a
Daniel score in a game where there was no such thing?
Why might he have done that? Elliot Binns[cxlvi] considers
Josephus' account of Alexander the Great in Jerusalem
a fabrication. He doesn't say why, but others suggest
that Josephus wanted to make Judaism look historically
important by an association with Alexander that never
happened. These are *Daniel* scholars who strive to put
its authorship in the second century BCE. So to admit
that Josephus' account of Alexander was accurate
would ruin their plot.

On the other hand, Tessa Rajak is a Josephus scholar
and writes with considerably more subtlety about

---

[66] Texting is a form of electronic communication popular during the first
decades of the twenty-first century.

Josephus' qualities as a historian than do Binns and others. Rajak says, for example, that

> interest seems to be declining in the critical question which has always dogged Josephus, the matter of his truthfulness... I felt it imperative to defend an often thoughtlessly maligned author... Josephus' accounts of the history and culture of his own day and age [are] not just evidence for reconstructing the situation, but as itself a large and fascinating and part of that history. *This made Josephus' inevitable and highly visible biases into a feature to be welcomed and exploited.*[cxlvii] (emphasis added)

The passage we discuss appeals to Josephus' bias in just such a way. Moreover, both Josephus and his sources needed the same bias for the *Daniel* element of the story to have come through intact. Callisthenes would not have had this Jewish bias.

The reader will have inferred long ere now that I am writing with an early-*Daniel* bias, so if I am right about the date of *Daniel* and can demonstrate that Josephus is generally an accurate historian and knows more about his subject matter than modern porphyrists, I am more than halfway home. And here the argument from silence is inappropriate: Josephus recorded it, and he may have been accurately reporting a historical event left out by others.

We have no extant contemporary accounts at all of Alexander's campaign, which is more like the sketchy Jones game in an old letter to a grandfather. All of the extant Alexander sources date from several centuries after the events; moreover, none makes an attempt to be comprehensive. Each includes events others omit.

Alexander had an official historian on his expedition, Callisthenes, nephew of Alexander's tutor Aristotle, the philosopher. Alexander executed Callisthenes for treason in 327 BCE, but this event was years before his execution. Callisthenes may have included this event. His obsequious *Deeds of Alexander* was published but is now lost. Nevertheless, it was still available in the first centuries of the Common Era and other ancient authors used it as a source of information. If Callisthenes or other early sources mentioned Alexander's visit to Jerusalem and the Temple, only Josephus chose to include the account, and Josephus' Jewish bias would have allowed him to include details that Callisthenes would not have understood or noted.

Let us analogize. When Hernando De Soto made the first exploration of mainland North America, landing on Florida's Gulf Coast in 1539, he had with him men who chronicled nearly every move the expedition made. We have their accounts translated for us in *The De Soto Chronicles*.[cxlviii] We are reasonably certain that De Soto was unaware of the Apalachee ceremonial mounds near the present Tallahassee because they are not mentioned. De Soto was as obsessive about the Native American cultus—notably, ceremonial mounds—as Alexander was about the temple cultus. De Soto visited every mound he knew about. The argument from silence is valid here for De Soto's campaign. Most important, the *Chronicles* survive with firsthand accounts of De Soto's expedition.

By contrast, even if Callisthenes' lost work were found and it mentioned the Jerusalem visit, he probably would not have given us the *Daniel* corroboration we are looking for. Callisthenes might have noted that Alexander visited the Temple in Jerusalem, might even have mentioned Alexander saying he had seen the Jewish priests in a dream, and still have omitted any reference to the book of *Daniel* as such: it was not in his frame of reference. He might have noted a predictive prophecy that we could have speculated was from *Daniel*, but with Josephus we have it spelled out for us. So even a corroboration of the visit to Jerusalem would likely not confirm the fourth-century copy (or possibly the autograph?) of the *Daniel* scroll seen there. Callisthenes could have been an eyewitness to the event and could have recorded the visit to the Temple, without noting that Alexander had been shown the book of *Daniel*.[67]

On the other hand, Jewish soldiers who joined Alexander's army, or the scribes and priests at the Temple, would have had the right kind of bias to remark on the *Daniel* episode on Alexander's visit to Judea; if they have written, they may have been Josephus' sources. Their accounts may be found someday. Or not.

---

[67] When someone finds a copy of Callisthenes and it says that Alexander was read a prophecy of his victory out of a Jewish holy book, I will say, "Oh my goodness! So I was wrong. How lovely!"

10
Alexander and Pliny the Elder

Josephus says that Alexander the Great visited the Temple in Jerusalem and was shown a copy of Daniel, and his prophecy that a Greek would defeat the Persians. The porphyrists say, "Tommyrot! Alexander never went to Jerusalem: Josephus was no historian, and just made it up." But there are various other extra-biblical evidences pointing to an Alexander trip into the interior of Judah, and one into Samaria, both tantalizingly close to Jerusalem. Let's look at them.

Ory Amitay addresses the argument from silence as it is used in reference to Alexander's campaign and how it might impact questions about Alexander's much-debated trip to Jerusalem.[cxlix] Amitay finds both a fairly healthy body of evidence against the validity of the argument from silence in the Alexandrian context ("Just because it isn't mentioned in the extant literature does not mean that it did not happen, in this case") and some plausible evidence that corroborates Josephus. Alexander must be in Jerusalem before (implicitly) seeing the book of *Daniel.*

Amitay says that since none of the accepted sources connects Alexander to Jerusalem or to the Hebrews, they seem at first glance to offer legitimate support for an argument from silence.[cl] Yet do they really? Even in the best sources, events are inexplicably omitted. Curtius tells one intriguing episode in full: "yet Arrian saw no place for it in his own work. What place would he find for a routine visit to a small temple town?[cli] Amitay notes several such instances in which the one historian describes an event while the other omits it. Nevertheless, Amitay manages to find a piece of evidence that places Alexander in Jerusalem with high probability, thanks to the balsam plant.

Alexander visited a balsam plantation in Jericho in about 332 BCE. Jericho is only seventeen miles from Jerusalem. This we shall see, with a little help from our friend Pliny.

Writers write about what interests them. Pliny the Elder (23–79 CE) was interested in all nature of things, including a wonderful kind of balsam, but not about the book of *Daniel* in the Temple at Jerusalem. This marvelous variety of the plant grew only in Judea and then only in two smallish gardens. It was used for perfumes and incense, as well as for medicinal balms.[68] The resin was highly prized and expensive. While other balsam was grown successfully in Italy and elsewhere, it never had the same potency as that grown at these Rift Valley plantations. I am interested in when *Daniel* was written. Our interest here in balsam is Pliny's mention of Alexander's presence at a balsam plantation, because it puts him near Jerusalem and ready to see *Daniel*, in about 332 BCE.

Pliny the Elder (Pliny the Younger was his nephew) was a Roman contemporary of Josephus who died in the

---

[68] The biblical Hebraic word for "balm" is *tzori*. The tzori, also used in incense, appears to have been the sap that drips from balsam trees.

aftermath of the eruption of Mt. Vesuvius in 79 CE. In one of his journals on agriculture and economics, he wrote about a remarkably valuable balsam crop that grew only in the Great Rift Valley at two plantations near the Dead Sea: one near Jericho just to the north, and the other at En Gedi, which overlooks the Dead Sea. It may be the altitude (the Dead Sea is 1,388 feet below sea level) that gives these plantations their balsam's potency.

En Gedi is the site of the cave where David restrained himself from killing King Saul, nearly seven hundred years earlier. Josephus tells us that the queen of Ethiopia had given David's son King Solomon the balsam root, which grows well near the Dead Sea.[clii] Perhaps that was the very beginning of this En Gedi enterprise, which apparently thrived for centuries before and after Alexander. Jericho (40 kilometers north of En Gedi) has been a well-established city since long before the time of Abraham and is one of the oldest settlements known to archaeology.

In Book XII of his *Natural History* (§LIV, 111), Pliny says,

> But every other scent ranks below balsam. The only country to which this plant has been vouchsafed is Judaea, where formerly it grew in only two gardens, both belonging to the king.[69]

And a few paragraphs later (§LIV, 117):

---

[69] Sed omnibus odoribus praefertur balsanum, uni terrarium iudaeae concessum, quondium in duobus tantum hortis, utroque regio,

> When Alexander the Great was conducting
> business there, it was an honest whole sum-
> mer day's work to fill one conch-shell [with
> the balsam nectar].[70]

We are not talking about a huge Florida horse conch, or even the slightly smaller fighting conch. These Judean shells were tiny—the size of a thumbnail. Pliny's Loeb editor, H. Rackham, notes the shell's volume: "The small *concha* was something over a hundredth part of a pint, the large *concha* three times that amount."[cliii],[71] What does Pliny mean by "when Alexander was conducting business there"? Was Alexander at one of the plantations himself, or did he send others? Pliny seems to indicate that he himself was there. (If so, it was probably Jericho—although for Alexander the 40 kilometers farther to En Gedi was apparently nothing if something interesting, such as the balsam, was at the end.)

Alexander had two reasons to investigate these balsam plantations in person. First, he had enormous personal curiosity about natural phenomena, which had probably been enhanced and nurtured by his tutor, the philosopher and polymath Aristotle. Second, the region of this industry would become his and would be tax-able, as soon as he had conquered Darius. Pliny continues (§118):

---

[70] Alexandro Magno res ibi gerente toto die aestivo unam concham impleri iustum erat, omni vero fecundidate e maiore horto congios senos, e minore singulos, cum et duplo rependebatur argento/argentum; nunc etiam singularum arborum largior vena. (Loeb edition, Rackham)

[71] I measured the capacity of a medium-sized Florida horse conch to hold sixteen ounces.

> for the entire produce of a rather large garden
> to be six *congii* (conch shells), and of a smaller
> one, one *congius*, at a time moreover when *its*
> *price was twice its weight in silver.* whereas today
> even a single tree produces a larger flow... There
> is a market for even the twigs; within five years
> of the conquest of Judea the actual loppings and
> twigs brought 800,000 sesterces. (emphasis added)

Pliny continues for several pages to wax enthusiastic over the virtues of the balsam, telling his audience both what can be done with the produce of the balsam and how to tell the pristine, unadulterated product from one that has been laced with other substances to fetch a better price. "In no other case is more obvious fraud practiced, inasmuch as every pint bought at a sale of confiscated property for 300 denarii when it is sold brings 1000 denarii" (§123). Such an industry, if run honestly and efficiently, can be quite valuable both for its owner and for the taxing au-thority. As potentially both owner and taxing authority, Alexander would have been interested indeed.

Pliny writes in the first century CE, nearly four hundred years after Alexander. How does he connect Alexander with the balsam plantations in Jericho and En Gedi? In the preface to his *Natural History*, Pliny says "You will count as proof of my professionalism the fact that I have prefaced these books with the names of my authorities."[cliv] It would mean much to the issue ultimately at hand—the date of *Daniel*—to find someone close to Alexander among these authorities from which Pliny gets his information about balsam nectar. Pliny doesn't make it easy, though. He lumps his sources at the very beginning, not correlating them with their citation. But for book XII of the *Natural History*, among the myriad sources listed is (drum roll and cymbal crash!) ... Callisthenes, Alexander's personal official chronicler![clv] His account was still extant when Pliny and Josephus wrote.

So in trying to tease out Alexander's activities in Judea and to determine Josephus' accuracy, placing Alexander where Binns and others say he never went, we are not left with their argument from silence. It is fair to say that only one of these extant sources—Josephus—puts Alexander in the vicinity of, or in, Jerusalem. But here we have Pliny, citing Callisthenes, putting him in Jericho, a mere seventeen miles away from Jerusalem itself. Callisthenes, probably an eyewitness, may have even mentioned his visit to the Temple (if not the *Daniel* episode).

Père Abel, who noted the potential implications of Pliny's statement,[clvi] wrote about a reconnaissance party led by Alexander, or by one of his generals, that left the shore and reached Jericho.[clvii] Both then and now one goes from Jerusalem to the Jordan "by the road to Jericho"—even in song. Jerusalem is between the Mediterranean and both of these two plantations, so a party going to either Jericho or En Gedi would normally travel through Jerusalem. It would make sense for Alexander to make an excursion to Jerusalem in the hill country and to the Rift Valley balsam plantations after the siege of Gaza, while he was recovering from a wound he incurred there and while he waited for cooler weather before taking his army across the Sinai desert.

We can tell from Pliny's accounts of the balsam plant that at least one of the lost first-generation Alexander histories discussed the properties of the balsam. Callisthenes fits the bill. Pliny's discussion of balsam connects with Alexander's actions in that geographical locale but was omitted by all but one of the authors mentioned above, of which none are firsthand accounts. Thus the argument from silence as an objection to Josephus' account is inappropriate here.

Josephus' account is written as early as any of the other extant accounts. Pliny's offhand remark about Alexander visiting a balsam plantation strengthens the credibility of Josephus' account of the event and thereby strengthens the argument for an early *Daniel*. Pliny's remark does not in itself prove that *Daniel* was written before Alexander died in 323 BCE, but it undermines the argument that it could not have happened, and strengthens Josephus' credibility.

There are two potential primary sources for Josephus' account of Alexander's being shown the passage about him in *Daniel*: soldiers and priests. Alexander allowed all the Jews in Judea, Babylon, and Media to enjoy their own laws. Moreover, they could enlist in his army continuing to obey the law of their forefathers, so many Jewish men joined his amy.[clviii]

Just as there were Macedonians and Greeks with Alexander who wrote their war stories, so probably Jewish enlistees would have chronicled their own stories of Alexander's army. We can postulate that the soldiers' written accounts, or the written records of Temple scribes who witnessed and took part in the event, probably would have included the showing of *Daniel* to Alexander, if that occurred.

If so, these Jewish accounts might have been where Josephus got his information. Speculative? Yes. Improbable? No. Both priests and soldiers would have had a cultural bias similar to that which Rajak attributes to Josephus. If some of them wrote, perhaps their texts have been preserved in clay jars somewhere. And if preserved, perhaps in a very dry cave. And if they have survived the 2,300 years in that cave (as some papyri have), one hopes, perhaps, someday they may be found. Found and made available for scholars and the rest of us.

11
Alexander in Samaria

Alexander came to the Samaritan highlands at least once, for a sadly dramatic purpose. He accomplished his purpose, and in doing so he contributed to Josephus' vindication as a historian. This vindication in turn undergirds Josephus' account of Alexander's seeing the book of *Daniel*.

In 1962 a tribe of Ta'amireh Bedouin discovered a cave in the Wadi ed-Daliyeh, a few miles north of Jericho, full of bat guano, human bones, pottery, and disintegrating papyrus scrolls. These cave findings further corroborate Josephus' accuracy as a historian. This archaeological discovery provides us with several pieces of our puzzle:

- It credits Josephus with knowing more about late-fourth-century history than his nineteenth- and twentieth-century detractors. The modern biblical historians thought Josephus was confused about a fourth century Samaritan ruler named Sanballat, whereas it was they who lacked Josephus' detailed information.
- It supports Curtius in placing Alexander in a part of Samaria tantalizingly close to Jericho, En Gedi, and Jerusalem. We need no longer have doubts about Alexander's being there himself, not merely sending others.
- It provides evidence for Alexander's preference for the Jewish nation over the Samaritans and

revises our date of the rift between the two cultures.

o   It corroborates a transfer of land from Samaria to Judea, thought by Josephus' critics to have been confused with a transfer centuries earlier.

Frank Moore Cross, Jr., American Dead Sea Scrolls and ancient languages scholar, tells the story succinctly:

> Evidence points to the last third of the fourth century B.C. for the abandonment of the series of late pre-Alexandrian documents and artifacts in the Daliyeh cave. A precise occasion for the dread event easily suggests itself. If Josephus is to be believed, the Samaritans initially ingrateated themselves with Alexander. Later while Alexander was in Egypt, Curtius reports, the Samaritans burned alive Andromachus, Alexander's Prefect in Syria. The act was not only a heinous crime, it was the first sign of revolt in Syria-Palestine, and *Alexander returned in all haste to Samaria, and according to Curtius took vengeance on the murderers who were "delivered up to him."*[clix] (emphasis added)

The Bedouin were the first to discover the execution scene, undisturbed except by bats and time, twenty-three centuries later. The forensic evidence at the scene fits well with Josephus' account of the external circumstances. Cross describes the scenario confirmed and elucidated by the findings in the cave in the Wadi ed-Daliyeh in the hills west of the Jordan River, a few miles north of Jericho.

After the rebellion that resulted in Andromachus' being burned alive, its leaders left the city when they heard that Alexander was approaching. They apparently ran for the hills with their families, food, and important papers, and hid in a cave to wait out the raid. But someone must have snitched on them and shown Alexander where they were hiding. And he knew what to do. The customary tactic for killing people hiding in a cave that has no rear entrance is to set a fire at the mouth of the cave, sucking the oxygen out and smothering them.

These Ta'amireh Bedouin had archaeological experience enough to recognize a likely place to dig through more than six feet of stinking bat guano. Their instincts paid off once more, and they discovered human bones, disintegrating woven mats, a gold ring, and enough disintegrating papyri to warrant taking samples to archaeologists. Cross tells us,

> One of the first items to come to our attention was a sealing affixed to the remnants of a papyrus inscribed in a clear Paleo-Hebrew script (not the Aramaic of the papyrus). It read: "...yaju, son of [San]ballat, governor of Samaria." There could be no doubt that, however fragmentary, the new find of papyri was of extraordinary importance.[clx]

We know Sanballat from *Nehemiah* 4:7 and following. *Nehemiah*'s Sanballat is a leader in the nations surrounding Judah conspiring against the Jewish returnees from Babylonia who were rebuilding the wall of Jerusalem. Modern scholars had assumed that Josephus' 'Sanballat', a contemporary of Alexander, must have been a colossal blunder: Josephus must have pulled him from *Nehemiah*,[clxi] the devious and malicious enemy of Nehemiah.

The evidence found in the Daliyeh cave changed several assumptions about biblical history and political history, and provided dated documents to tabulate the carbon dating of fourth-century papyri. It also, incidentally, placed Alexander the Great again in the close vicinity of Jerusalem. Momigliano, Binns and others should not be quite so sure that Alexander was never in Jerusalem.

Scholars had assumed Josephus had no sense of historical accuracy and could not be trusted for information they didn't already have. But a cave at ed Daliyeh provided evidence of another Sanballat. Josephus knows more about extra-biblical history than modern scholars! Here in this Samaritan cave, experts in ancient Semitic languages found a trove of papyri.

> The range of dates extends from about 375 B.C. down to 335 B.C. The range covers one of the darkest eras in the history of Palestine.[clxii] ...The content of all the papyri is legal or administrative.[clxiii]

The ringleaders of the insurrection against Alexander fled with their families and administrative papers to the cave, where they all perished. Cross says that this gives us information where we had little before, so we can now reconstruct with some plausibility the sequence of governors of Samaria in the fifth and fourth centuries. These papyri provide us with missing information and with clues that fill significant gaps.

For solving the mystery of the *Daniel* Hoax, we are not so much interested in showing that Alexander was present at the Daliyeh cave as in showing that Josephus knew whereof he wrote as a historian *par excellence*. If he is accurate here, in the face of modern skepticism, he is less vulnerable to the infection of a tainted reputation. Showing Alexander in Samaria is icing on the cake.

We now have Cross's reconstruction of Samaritan rulers:

- o Fifth century, Sanballat I, the Horonite and nemesis of Nehemiah
- o Sanballat II, early fourth century (in the Daliyeh papyri), whom Cross hypothesizes may have been the grandson of Sanballat I and father-in-law of Jesus, killed in the Temple by his brother Johanan (Josephus, *Antiquities* xi.297–301)
- o His son Yeshua (?), succeeded his brother Hananiah, governor by 353
- o Sanballat III, appointed by Darius III, and governor of Samaria when Alexander the Great became ruler

Other scholars have tweaked Cross's reconstruction. Even so, Josephus is vindicated here. It now becomes plausible that there were Sanballats in Samaria for several generations, just as there were Louises in France, Henrys in England, and Dariuses in Medo-Persia. What seemed to be Josephus' confusion of parallel marriages between Jews and Samaritans in generations a century apart brought scorn from modern scholars. With undisguised irony Cross notes Cowley's analysis:

> The view that there were two Sanballats, each governor of Samaria, and each with a daughter who married a brother of a High Priest at Jerusalem is a solution too desperate to be entertained.[clxiv]

Ha! With the evidence from the Daliyeh papyri, we now may entertain that solution with nary a drop of desperation. In fact, these papyri completely change what we had assumed about that portion of our universe of information. They require a rewrite of a period of history.

Scholars had assumed that the schism between Samaria and Judea began with the return of the Jews from Babylon. But the Daliyeh papyri give concrete evidence that cordiality and marriages continued during the intervening century. The Daliyeh papyri, alongside Curtius and Josephus, testify that the schism between Samaritans and Jews did not occur until the time of Alexander, rather than more than two centuries earlier, as had been thought. This schism may or may not have been complete at this time. Beckwith says that it was not until two hundred years later that the schism became final:

> It is now known that the Samaritans continued to follow Jewish customs long after the time of Ezra and Nehemiah, and that the schism did not become complete until the Jews destroyed the Samaritan temple on Mount Gerizim about 110 BC. It seems that the Samaritans only then rejected the Prophets and the Writings because of the recognition of those books give to the temple at Jerusalem.[clxv]

Other scholars put the schism at the time of Alexander, over a land transfer. Hence is earlier than Beckwith's event, based on the Jewish destruction of the Samaritan temple, but later than the traditional Nehemiah period. The precise date is only tangential to the dating of *Daniel*, but it has a particular impact on the dating of the OT canon. This obscure period of history is marginally revealed by the Daliyeh papyri.

We should no longer be as inclined to discount automatically everything Josephus writes. It appears that Alexander himself led the search party that suffocated the Samaritans in the cave. So it may have occasioned a second visit to Jerusalem. Josephus says that his initial visit to the Temple was soon after his conquest of Gaza, and before his trip to Egypt. Alexander got news of the insurrection and death of his prefect Andromachus in Egypt, so this trip would have been later than his first Temple visit.

Alexander's retribution mission to Samaria could also have included the trip to the balsam plantations in Jericho, a mere 16 kilometers to the south of Ed Daliyeh and another 40 to En Gedi, or they could have been separate trips. They could easily have occurred at any time between the victory at Issus in late October or early November 333 BCE and his arrival in Mesopotamia some two years later. If he had not already made the visit to the Temple, either the Samaria mission or the balsam visit would have inspired, nay demanded, a little side trip to see the Temple in Jerusalem.

In a meticulously constructed study of Alexander's movements in the area, Aryeh Kasher gives us a plausible rationale for Alexander's itinerary during this period.[clxvi] After the conquest of Tyre (summer 332), Alexander appointed Andromachus as prefect of Coele-Syria. Kasher quotes Abel[clxvii] as inferring from Pliny the Elder (re balsam plantations) that he went to Jericho while Tyre was under siege.

The Daliyeh trip cannot have been in 332, though, because Andromachus had not even been appointed, much less killed. So we now seem to have possible evidence of three separate visits of Alexander into the interior, where scholars thought there had been none:

- o 332, first half, during siege of Tyre: the visit to Jericho for the balsam plantations (Abel, Gutman, Kasher)
- o 332, autumn, after siege of Gaza: visit to Jerusalem, Temple (Josephus)
- o 331 Egypt, news of Samarian insurrection, goes to Samaria and ed-Daliyeh (Kasher)

This is not to say that there could not have been more; he could have visited balsam plantations or the Temple several times, and there were many likely opportunities. A siege can be boring.

So Alexander now has at least two incursions into the Judean hill country—one to check out the balsam industry, the other to avenge the death of his prefect by the Samaritans—and on either trip he could have stopped off at Jerusalem to visit the Temple. Or he could plausibly have made several trips specifically to visit the Temple.

Or none at all? Ari Belenkiy[clxviii] suggests that Josephus conflated the Alexander the Great meeting with the high priest with a meeting of Antiochus III the Great with Simon the Just—not Alexander and Jaddua, but Antiochus and Simon. In both instances, the rulers were surrendering Jerusalem to Greece. The Alexander event occurred in 332 BCE, the Antiochus meeting in 199 BCE.

Were there two events or only one? One of the conceits of modern biblical scholarship is to assume that if there are two events in the Bible that are similar, there must actually have been only one (if one), and that one of the events is sloppy historianship. The Talmud (B. Yoma,

69a) calls the high priest in the Alexander event Simon the Just (210–196 BCE), and that may be the site of the conflation rather than Josephus, because Simon's dates are wrong for Alexander. Josephus says that the high priest was Jaddua (335–320 BCE, with appropriate dates).

Belenkiy assumes that there was only one event, and that it was between Antiochus and Simon in about 199 BCE. But it is likely in this case (and perhaps in most cases) that more than one similar event happened. Belenkiy marshals several points in support of his claim that the Alexander meeting with the priests at the Temple never occurred. For example, there is a rabbinical story about the Jews promising to name their sons for the conqueror during the next year. Belenkiy goes about researching this in an appropriate way—by looking at the names of ordinary people. Do we find a time when there were several Jewish boys named Antiochus? Alexander? Belenkiy finds an 'Antiochus' from about the right period, but no 'Alexanders'. Belenkiy points out that Alexander's popularity in Judea peaked at a time when Antiochus was unpopular, so the story morphed over to Alexander, a better hero of the moment. I suggest that both stories could have happened.

Belenkiy says that there are other biblical books Antiochus could have been shown over which he would have been pleased, as Alexander was pleased with the prophecy in *Daniel*. I will gladly grant him that.

And then there is the Mt. Scopus issue. Belenkiy says that the conqueror in question must have been entering Jerusalem from Mt. Scopus, from which he could have observed the rising of the star Canopus, a natural phenomenon that confirmed the curvature of the earth (of interest to Alexander as a scientific curiosity). But Alexander would have been entering from the Jaffa road and not seen Canopus. But it is even more likely that Alexander could have come from Daliyeh or the Jericho or Ein Gedi balsam plantations by the Jericho road, and would have have passed Mt. Scopus.

Belenkiy says that Alexander, as a student of Aristotle, already knew that the earth was round and would not have been impressed to see the rising of Canopus. But that is not typical. Alexander would probably have been quite interested: people love to find evidence for something they already know to be true, especially if they have trouble persuading others of it. To find a place from which to see a star that proved the earth is round would have delighted Alexander.

Belenkiy attempts to make a firm resolution of the problem—to put the notion to rest, once and for all, that Alexander did not visit Jerusalem.

Methinks he doth protest too much.

12
Daniel Elsewhere

Evidence of Alexander's excursions into the hill country and the Jordan valley advances our quest in two ways. It vindicates our trust in the evidence we have from Josephus. Because he knew the political history of Samaria and confounded the twentieth-century scholars regarding details of Sanballat, the Samaritan temple, and other tidbits, he may also be right about the priests showing the *Daniel* scroll to Alexander. It also puts Alexander in a geographical position for this to have happened in or about the year 331 BCE, more than a century and a half before most theological scholars think *Daniel* was written.

In Elliot Binns's rehearsal of issues he supports a second century dating of *Daniel*,[clxix] he claims complete omission of any mention of *Daniel* in the Jewish literature before the second century. But this charge requires some special pleading. Let's consider instances where there is either outright mention of Daniel the man or an implicit inference that the book was already known.

We have discussed at exhaustive length *Ezekiel*'s mentions of Daniel the man. Pusey cites eight other references, allusions, and passages that make no sense without the book of *Daniel* being already prominent in the literature.[clxx] So next we catalogue *Daniel* references in the work of authors writing before or during the Maccabean period.

Nehemiah. First the critics urged that if the historical Daniel had written *Daniel*, it would have been referenced in later biblical books. Then when these critics find such a reference, as in *Nehemiah*, they quietly assume as self-evident that the prayer at *Daniel* 9:4–19 was copied from the one in *Nehemiah*, not the other way round.[clxxi] So they commit the fallacy of begging the question: they present as evidence what they should be trying to prove. Which came first, *Daniel* or *Nehemiah*? Who copied whom?

Pusey says that perhaps neither did. The background is this: Cyrus, the king of the Medo-Persians, conquered Babylon in 538 BCE and decreed that Babylonia's captive peoples could go back to their respective countries, be more productive in their own lands, and send him lots of tribute money. Daniel would have been by then nearly eighty years old. Nehemiah, a generation or two younger than Daniel, was one of the leaders of those who eventually went back to Jerusalem to rebuild the city wall.

Nehemiah no doubt had heard of Nebuchadnezzar and Daniel, his Jewish prime minister, and perhaps he may have known or met Daniel personally as Cyrus' advisor. Would he have been influenced by his famous compatriot's words? Or conversely would a pseudo-Daniel, writing in the second century BCE, have been influenced by the scriptural words of the prophet Nehemiah? Just from those facts, it seems a toss-up. So perhaps Pusey is right: neither copied the other.

The two prayers are at *Daniel* (9:4–19) and at *Nehemiah* (9:5–38). The prayers are both old-fashioned. But if these prayers had been included in writing assignments of two of my students, I would not question either of them about plagiarism. They are simply not that much alike, given that both authors are of the same religion and culture and are writing in roughly the same time period. Pusey agrees—or at least I agree with Pusey. He notes that the opponents of the early dating of *Daniel* have exaggerated any correspondence between the prayers. He says that nothing could be less alike than these two prayers, except insofar as both confess the sins of the people and beseech God's forgiveness. That is the way we are all supposed to pray: "Forgive us our trespasses". I allow that they both address the Almighty in a similar fashion, but that is a matter of cultural practice. It would have been odd indeed if either had addressed his prayer to his "Dear Heavenly Father" or "Abba".

But Pusey points out that *Nehemiah*'s prayer rehearses historical facts.

> It is a confession of God's mercies from the call of Abraham ...ending with a profession of amendment. It proceeds in one steady unbroken course of narrative, from first to last. It contains scarcely a petition ... [except] *let not all the trouble seem little to Thee, which hath come upon us* ... Throughout that part of the prayer which relates to the history in the Pentateuch, idioms and sentences of the Pentateuch are worked in; even the precise words [of the Pentateuch] are retained ... In the same way in which he used the language of the Pentateuch and of other earlier Scripture, [Nehemiah] also used language of Daniel's prayer.[clxxii]

Pusey goes on to point out that *Daniel*'s prayer is rhetorical, not historical. It is one eloquent, fervid, tide of prayer, rising and falling in a prolonged cadence, as it sets forth successively God's faithfulness, man's unfaithfulness; God's righteousness, man's unrighteousness; God's mercy, man's sinfulness calling down God's justice; then an impassioned gush of ..."Lord, tarry not, Lord, hearken and do" overcomes God, and Daniel's prayer is answered.[clxxiii]

No one, Pusey concludes, could doubt which had used the language of the other. 'Nehemiah' could naturally allude only to language of *Daniel*; his history had no natural bearing on *Daniel*'s history or prophecies.[clxxiv]

Zechariah's Horns. Two of *Zechariah*'s visions presuppose *Daniel*'s prophecy of the four empires and are very obscure unless 'Zechariah' can assume that his audience is familiar with *Daniel*. *Zechariah* says in chapter 1:18,

> Then I raised my eyes and looked and there were four horns. [19] And I said to the angel who talked with me, "What are these?" And he answered me, "These are the horns that have scattered Judah, Israel, and Jerusalem."

Now where have we seen four horns before this? In *Daniel*, of course. At 8.15 the speaker identifies himself as "I, Daniel". He then tells of a vision of a ram. He hears a voice off stage telling a holy one who was there, "Gabriel, make this man understand the vision." There was a ram with two horns, one higher than the other, identified in verse 20 as the kings of Media and Persia. It was slain by a shaggy he-goat (Greece, v. 21). Then the he-goat's one large horn was broken:

> The goat became very great, but at the height

> of his power the horn between his eyes
> broke off and in its place *four prominent
> horns* grew up toward the four winds of
> heaven. (8:8) (emphasis added)

Alexander died at the height of his power with no heir, and his empire was divided among four of his generals. Without the he-goat story in *Daniel*, *Zechariah*'s horns make very little sense. The nations represented by the four horns did indeed scatter Judah, Israel, and Jerusalem. Everybody knew *Daniel* and recognized the horns.

Zechariah's Chariots. The next reference to *Daniel* is at Zechariah 6:1–3, where he has four chariots come from between two bronze mountains. Pusey explains:

> The same four-fold division of power recurs
> in the vision of the four chariots which issue
> from between the two mountains of brass,
> with horses red, black, white, grizzled, strong.
> Those who have not explained this vision by
> aid of Daniel's four world-empires have been
> puzzled, (1) why the title *strong* should have
> been given to one set only of these symbols
> of power;[72] (2) why, in the explanation of the
> Angel, the first symbol, the chariot with the
> *red* horses, disappears. Four symbols of earthly
> power are exhibited to the prophet; three only
> are explained. Obviously, since the symbols
> represent the same as in Daniel, there was no-
> thing to be said about the first monarchy;
> for it was gone. Of the black horses, then it is

---

[72] Perhaps those who are puzzled have read the Revised Standard Version, which calls the last chariot's horses 'dappled gray', reminding many readers of the boy who "had a little pony, they called him dappled grey . . ." and not the 'grizzled' or 'strongly grizzled' that Pusey suggests.

> said, *they have made my anger to rest on the North
> country,* i.e., on Babylon, of which the former
> prophets had ever spoken, as *the North.* The
> third, it is said, *go forth after them,* for the Greek
> empire occupied the same portion of the earth
> as the Persian. The fourth, the Roman, is desig-
> nated by the grizzled and strong horses, corres-
> ponding to those characteristics of strength and
> mingled character, so prominent in the fourth
> empire in Daniel.[clxxv]

With the help of Pusey's commentary, it is easier to
relate *Zech-ariah*'s visions to those of *Daniel.* I had first
envisioned *Zechariah*'s chariots coming out together,
side by side. With Pusey's help, I realize they are coming one after the other, and are indeed either the same
empires as in *Daniel* chapters 2 and 6, or the four
kingdoms of the he-goat's generals.

It is the nature of genuine prophecy to be vague. So
here the four empires alternatively could be simply the
kingdoms under the four generals of Alexander, and the
strongly grizzled horses would represent Ptolemaic
Egypt. At any rate, Zechariah gives us very little eluci-
dation with-out *Daniel*'s four horns.

Maccabees. Pusey also cites the extreme accuracy of
the first book of *Maccabees.* This was written about 165
BCE and is an exact but simple reference to the book
of *Daniel.* There is great precision in the father of the
Maccabean heroes, Mattathias, saying to his sons on his
deathbed:

> Hananiah, Azariah, and Mishael [Shadrach,
> Mishach, and Abednego] had faith, and they
> were saved from the blazing furnace. Daniel

> was a man of integrity, and he was rescued
> from the lions' jaws. (2:59–60)

Mattathias' sons would not have distorted his dying words. He speaks of Daniel as historical hero. He would not have admired the fictional hero of a contemporary novel written by a 'Daniel' whom he knew to be a pseudepigrapher who only pretended high office, heroics, and prophetic visions.

The Septuagint. The LXX translation of the Pentateuch is dated no later than Ptolemy Philadelphus, ruler of Egypt 285–246 BCE. Here *Deuteronomy* 32:8 is rendered as, "When the Most High divided the nations, when He dispersed the sons of Adam, He established the bounds of the nations according to *the number of the angels of God*," instead of *"the number of the children of Israel",* as in the Masoretic Text.

This introduces into the LXX the doctrine that angels are guardians over the several nations, a doctrine which is nowhere found except in *Daniel.*[clxxvi] This brings angels into the Pentateuchal economy, an idea first seen in *Daniel,* and places the authorship of *Daniel* before the third-century BCE Septuagint. There was probably a considerable time between the writing of *Daniel* and its translation into the Greek of the LXX.

Baruch's Prayer. Pusey notes that the prayer of Baruch is a mosaic, formed of jewels from Daniel, Nehemiah, and Jeremiah, blended together yet not forming one distinct whole.[clxxvii] Of the *Daniel* portion, porphyrists have suggested mere coincidence—that both authors had used formulae then in general use, and also that 'Daniel' must have copied *Baruch.* Pusey protests that *Baruch*'s version is an expansion of *Daniel* each time, and that the agreement is not formulaic, but in whole verses, even in the same order. He then notes a comparison of the two:

Daniel	Baruch
9:7 O Lord, the right is on your side, the shame on ours	1:15 The Lord is in the right; on us the shame
9:8 The shame is ours and our king's, princes', forefathers'	1:16 The shame on the men of Judah, our rulers, priests, fathers
9:10 We have not obeyed the Lord, his laws, prophets	1:21 We refused to hear the Lord speaking in the prophets
9:11 All Israel has broken thy law, disobeyed thee. Curses on us	1:20 We are suffering under the curse Moses pronounced
9:12 He has fulfilled, bringing calamity on Jerusalem	2:1,2 fulfilling the law, nowhere such deeds as in Jerusalem
9:13 foreshadowed in the law of Moses, this calamity	2:8 the Lord brought on us this evil, because he is just
etc.	etc.

It is obvious that 'Daniel' has not only the better turn of phrase, but the more forthright way of expressing it. The literary genius also has the original insight. The leader in insight also, at least here, leads in its expression.

13
The Theology of Porphyrism

In the context of the present study, the only stance that is labeled 'porphyrism' is the claim that predictive prophecy is impossible. Its corollary here is that Daniel is a hoax, which we go to enormous lengths to disprove. In principle, a porphyrist could profess any religion to which he or she was drawn. But theology is subject to logical constraints such as a premise that states "if x then not-y". So in this chapter we examine some of these in terms of porphyrism.

Many people make a couple of standard mistakes about miracles. They insist that if events are real, they should be repeatable. That is the way science works, isn't it? If other scientists cannot repeat a scientific event such as a chemical synthesis or an atom smash, then it was some kind of fluke and doesn't count. But God's miracles are one-off events. Similarly, people sometimes conflate biblical prophecy with non-biblical forms of foretelling, a behavior that is strictly proscribed by the Bible, which disallows the claims of fortune-tellers, sooth-sayers, the readers of entrails, astrologers, idolaters, and anyone else who claims to manipulate some kind of power to tell the future or to guide the future. God forbids his people from having anything to do with such.

That said, the claim that predictive prophecy in the Bible is both possible and legitimate is based on the following premises:

> Predictive prophecy is necessarily the action of God, who is sovereign over everything that is, was, and is to be.
> God's sovereignty includes what in human limitation is referred to as 'time'.
> God is good, and he works things together to benefit those of his creatures who acknowledge his sovereignty and his goodness. (Ro 8.28)
> God is able to communicate with, and convey information to, those human beings who acknowledge his sovereignty and goodness.

But many porphyrists fail to distinguish unbiblical claims from those of the God of the Bible. Hence porphyrists consider the supposed foretellings in *Daniel* (and elsewhere in the Bible) always and necessarily to be prophecy-after-the-fact. They are caught in various sorts of logical binds that are often a failure to distinguish false prophets from prophets of the sovereign God, who can tell the future because he creates the future. So porphyrism has theological consequences.

Take atheism. If the porphyrist is an avowed atheist, he is at least self-consistent up to a point. He believes that there is no such being as God, that everything in the universe is a result of chance, and that consequently the future is necessarily indeterminate: it hasn't happened yet. Therefore he holds that nobody can tell the future. We can agree with the atheist that if God didn't exist, and were not the creator of everything, it would be impossible for anyone to tell the future, because it is God who makes the future happen. With no God the whole of everything would be a crapshoot.

Most atheists assume that what they can believe in is all there is. For example, many believe that death brings "a final oblivion with no accountability," as C. FitzSimons Allison puts it.[clxxviii] Many people who commit suicide are lulled by that assumption into killing themselves— "I will just go to sleep and escape from the problems that are troubling me here in this life."

But Shakespeare—that perceptive observer of the human condition—gives that fantasy the slip. We cannot see or measure the content of one another's thoughts, or dreams, or deaths. Ol' Will has Hamlet say, "To be, or not to be?"—that is, "to live, or to die?" Death looks like a dreamless sleep, but is it dreamless?

>To die, to sleep,
>To sleep, perchance to dream;

And then he suggests (as we all know) that dreams are not always pleasant: some dreams are a whole lot like hell.

>Aye, there's the rub;
>For in that sleep of death,
>>what dreams may come when we have
>>shuffled off this mortal coil must give us pause. .
>. . .the dread of something after death,
>the undiscovered Country
>>from whose bourn no Traveller returns,
>Puzzles the will
>>and makes us rather bear the ills we have
>>than fly to others that we know not of.
>Thus conscience does make Cowards of us all.[clxxix]

Oh that some of our atheist friends who have flown via suicide to that undiscovered Country from whose bourn no Traveller returns had had enough of Hamlet's foreboding to be Cowards! Believing that there is no God doesn't make it so. Wake up and smell the sulphur? No, no, my friend! Change your mind before it's too late! What any of us believes has no effect on some things: taxes, predictive prophecy, death ... Don't do it!

Wouldn't it be wonderful if not believing in taxes, or cancer, would make them go away, wonderful if believing that death is a pleasant nothingness would make it so! If it were so, we might quickly emulate Lewis Carroll's queen and practice believing that cancer and taxes and hell don't exist. We could practice believing in several other things before breakfast each morning, and have our choice of which things to make go away.

But no. Somebody said memorably that we are entitled to our own opinions, but we are not entitled to our own facts. We and atheists are all dealing here with cosmic reality—weather, gravity, the forces of good and evil—and we are either right or wrong. Anyone's belief here is irrelevant as to whether we are right or wrong. So be ye Cowardly! Death and eternity are facts we cannot manipulate.

Hence the atheist who believes that there can be no genuine predictive prophecy is simply confused because his belief is irrelevant. He assumes *a priori* that predicttion is impossible, because he prefers to believe that God doesn't exist. He lets his standards of evidence become overwhelmed by this *a priori* assumption, so that any evidence that contradicts this belief must be swept under the rug—somehow explained away.

I wish I could say that it puzzles me why porphyrists are eager to endorse the Rapha-Man. They believe that he is Ezekiel's Daniel despite a pivotal part of his story's plot hinging on idols. They believe in the raphe-Man's visions, and their power to confer fecundity, when these same porphyrists are equally eager to fault Josephus for his accounts of Alexander's prophetic dream and Daniel's prophetic visions.

Most porphyrists fail to be equal-opportunity scoffers: Theoretically, they don't believe in any of the gods, Daniel's or Danel's. The porphyrist thinks that both Danel the Rapha-Man and Daniel the Prime Minister of Babylon are fictional or mythical. But they fervently believe that the story of the Rapha-Man must be a part of Hebrew folk memory for more than half a millennium, so that Ezekiel can resurrect him in his diatribe against the Prince of Tyre, and in his sermon to the idol-worshipping Jewish elders.

This means that to an atheist the rules of evidence don't really apply. The same standards the porphyrist applies to some of the *Psalms* scrolls and fragments found at Qumran are not allowed to apply to the *Daniel* scrolls and fragments also found there. He ignores the evidence that 'Daniel' knew whereof he spoke about Belshazzar and condemns *Daniel* as a hoax because no one has as yet produced similar evidence explaining Darius.

But there are porphyrists who are not atheists. Some are churchgoers and preachers. To admittedly oversimplify and overcategorize, let's pretend for the moment that there are only three general varieties of porphyrist churchgoers: panentheists, deists, and theists. The first two deceive themselves into thinking that God does not engage his prophets in predictive prophecy.

Unlike the atheist, the panentheist believes in a God who changes as his universe evolves. Pan*en*theism differs from simple, old-fashioned pantheism, which holds that all things are God or Gods, so that the divine interpenetrates all of the universe. Panentheism's God is not limited to the universe, as is pantheism's, but is its animating force. Hasidic Judaism and Hinduism both have elements of panentheism, as does the Baha'i faith. The philosopher Charles Hartshorne's Process Theology is panentheistic. The element of panentheism that is not compatible with predictive prophecy is its God, who is changing with the universe as he is creating it, but who does not interact with it in the sense of becoming human (i.e., Jesus) or appearing as a man at Mamre, or sending angels upon occasion to speak with his creatures.

A panentheistic God is part of the evolving universe, and is not sovereign over it, nor does he sovereignly direct its course of evolution. So he cannot predict its future. Just as with atheism, believing in panentheism does not make it so. God changes not, his compassions they fail not. As he has been he forever will be. Great is his faithfulness.[clxxx]

Other porphyristic church-goers may be deists. Their God is immutable, but they may be more confused than the atheists and panentheists. There are two kinds of deists: those whom some call Double-Dogged Determinists and those whose God is the Clockmaker. The former believe that the universe was set in motion at the beginning (by a creator or by chance), and every step of the development of the universe follows in its every aspect from the prior configurations of the universe. Thus I am sitting here typing on my laptop, not free to do anything else. Every letter I type and every mistake I make was determined from the moment of the Big Bang. We and Heisenberg are all helpless to change an atom, indeterminacy or not. Some people wrongly interpret Calvinism as if Calvin espoused this view.

Other deists believe in a Clockmaker God who designs a clockwork universe, winds it up, and sets it in motion. But once started, he can change nothing, but only call from the sidelines and ask his prophets to forthtell—to yell lusty platitudes. The deist's God cannot construct the future: he already did that at the beginning of time. He has set the whole thing in motion, so now he can only watch it play out the instructions he gave it. He *knows* the future and is perfectly able to tell the future to his prophets. But neither his foretelling the future nor their forthtellings can change history. It is what it is. Things can go wrong with his handiwork, but he must stand by helpless as it runs down.

The deistic universe has a Cassandra Complex. You remember that the god Apollo gave Cassandra, daughter of King Priam of Troy, the gift of prophecy, but with one flaw: nobody ever believed or heeded her prophecies. "Don't step on a crack! You'll break your mother's back!" but everybody steps on cracks anyway, and all the old ladies develop osteoporosis. (Now that we know the cause of osteoporosis, you'd think we could persuade the general populace to quit stepping on cracks. But a deistic world can change nothing.) Only if the deist God has programmed into his universe at the

beginning a prophet's foretelling an accurate future can
his prophet predict. So the deist God is compatible
with both porphyrism and prediction, insofar as he has
programmed either into his universe. His adherents
don't bother to believe in predictive prophecy, because
they think that doing so doesn't make a hill of beans.
They ignore their God with equanimity—why not? It is
the easiest way to behave.

Both the Determinist deity and the Clockmaker deity
inspire porphyrism because although the deist's God
knows the future, and may have programmed some of
the people of his universe to be predictive prophets,
prophecy isn't much fun in his universe. It can be right
on the money every time, but nobody will change their
bets or their behavior. The whole kabuki is simply the
playing out of a future that the deity set in motion.

Deists say the creeds in church—avowing that they
believe in a God who is "almighty, maker of heaven
and earth and all things visible and invisible, seen and
unseen". But for deists, God is helpless to right
wrongs. And again, believing in deism does not make it
so.

Theism, on the third hand, believes in a God who is
sovereign over every instant of his universe. Unlike the
deist's God, the theist's God often reveals himself in
predictive prophecy. He enables his prophets in both
foretelling and forthtelling for the purpose of persuading mankind to forsake his wicked ways, to turn to God
and live.

The deist's God's future is as the past, unchangeable. The theist's God is the one we talk about in the creeds, who makes all things and keeps them going. He not only created the universe and all that is, but he continually creates it. None of us could draw our next breath without God, the Creator, in which we each breathe and move and have our being. He doesn't just know the future as we know the end of a novel we have read. He knows the future more like we know the end of a novel we are writing. He makes everything happen in accordance with his will.

We may prefer the (illusory) self-control of the deist, whose God made the universe, saw that it was good, and then went off and played a round of golf. Go away, God! We don't like someone who knows all about us, hovering around and getting in our way. Go mind your own business, God; make yourself a new galaxy, but don't keep telling us what to do, and especially what not to do. Clockmaker deities are very popular with modernists. Thomas Jefferson was a deist; Ben Franklin would have been if he had had any God at all. It is easy to trust in a God who has done his job and left. Creation? Check: Done that. See? Universe! Tah, I'm off. See ya!

But it takes the sovereign God of the theists to make a universe where the Creator is in complete control. He creates complex beings whose chief objective in life is to honor and worship him, but who have the freedom to ignore him or reject him. The fact of the matter is that either God exists—with the whole sovereignty package—or he doesn't. And we exist, don't we?— freedom, sins and all? It is he who hath made us, and

not we ourselves. (Psalm 100) Either there is a sovereign God who directed Daniel's life and writing, or
there is no such being.

It is not the case that one person has a sovereign God
and the next person has some other kind of God or no
God at all. We all have the same God, sovereign over
us and everyone else. So we had better get used to it.

God's to-do list: Make creatures. Check. Make them
able to love me or not love me. Persuade them to love
me in spite of being inclined to love themselves instead
of me. Hmmm. Not automatically. No fun if they were
a bunch of robots. Send the Son to show them how.
Check. Write *Psalm* 22 five hundred years ahead of time
to tell them precisely how things are going to happen.
Check. Write a slew of other predictions about my
plans for them. Check. Make those things happen.
Check. Allow creatures to disbelieve; let them be
atheists or panentheists or deists. If they don't love me
and don't want to play on my turf, let them spend
eternity away from me. Check.

John N. Oswalt, in his commentary on *Isaiah*, tells us
that any self-consistent theist should accept foretelling
as part of the prophetic package. "It is not hard to imagine," Oswalt says, "why a thoroughgoing naturalist
[i.e., an atheist] would take a position against foretelling." The atheist has no sovereign God by means of
which these predictions could come. But it is much
more difficult to imagine why modern theologians and
commentators, most of whom consider themselves at
least theists, if not supernaturalists, would hold such a
view. Surely if there is such a God, omnipotent and

omniscient, and if he is able to make special knowledge about *himself* available to his messengers for them to forthtell, it is no great feat to make special knowledge about the *future* available to these messengers for them to foretell.[clxxxi] The theist's God can make his prophets both foretell the future and forthtell his will. Hence on Oswalt's view, and on my own, if there is no foretelling, then there is no forthtelling either. The deist's God can run along the sidelines and shout instructions to his team, but even if one of his players happens to forthtell his God's instructions, nobody changes the plays they were destined from the beginning of time to make, so the score is the same whether or not anybody foretold anything or not. No sovereign God, no effective mouthpiece. Isn't it wonderful that the Deist's thinking doesn't make it so! Or the Panentheist's, or the Atheist's!

As far as that goes, the theist's thinking does not make for a sovereign God, either. He exists and is in control, or not. Our thinking does not make it so, any more than our not believing in him does not make him not so. His being is independent of us, despite our petty pridefulness. But our choice to believe or not to believe has consequences. We necessarily choose. Refusing to choose—calling ourselves agnostic—is choosing not to believe in him. What are our odds? Fifty fifty? Not on your life! Read Pascal's Wager, or my little book *God's Odds*, reprising Pascal, and if you bet the wrong way, it will not be without knowing the odds against you. Don't spend your baby's milk money on a lottery ticket!

Hooray for a God who is in control of everything and is benevolent, and knows better than I do what is good for me!

God is who he is—creator and ruler of all—and he is who *Daniel* says he is. We should rejoice and be exceedingly glad because all shall be well, and all shall be well, and all manner of thing shall be well.[73]

Why do the porphyrists so furiously rage?

[73] With thanks to the insight of Mother Julian of Norwich.

14
In the Drawing Room, Please

Ahem. Please take your seats. I have invited you all, and my colleagues Miss Jane Marple and M. Hercule Poirot, to gather here this evening to discuss the puzzling events we confront surrounding our friend, the much-beloved Daniel, who became prime minister of Babylon. There has been scurrilous talk for more than a century, charging that his life work has been a hoax. Not only that his work has been a hoax, but that he himself never existed, that he is a phantasm emanating from the imagination of a political hack who wrote in Jerusalem at the time of the Maccabees. They are of course dead wrong!

We are gathered here tonight to rescue our friend from the prison of ignominy to which Theological Academia has relegated him, to put their charges to rest, and to place the eminent Daniel's reputation back on the pedestal it so well deserves.

Most modern critics list no reasons at all for assigning a late date to *Daniel*. They just know that it is late because that is what they have been taught by their elders. They vainly seek information about Babylon in *Second Isaiah*,[74] which they think was written during the Babylonian exile, also without evidence except their prejudice

---

[74] There is no *Second Isaiah*. One author wrote the entire book. But that is a subject for another time, another tome.

against a misguided analysis of *Isaiah*'s predictive prophecy. Here they find a man going into a forest. Babylonia was unforested, whereas Israel and Judah had areas that were heavily forested in the eighth century BCE when 'Isaiah' wrote. 'Isaiah' was not in Babylon, but in Judea. 'Daniel' was in Babylon, and knew whereof he wrote.

And then there is Belshazzar. Early nineteenth-century porphyrists thought that a second-century 'Daniel' had invented him because the assumed hoaxer didn't know anything about Babylon during the exilic period. Then, lo and behold, Belshazzar appeared in 1854 when four little cylinders with cuneiform writing were found in a ziggurat in Ur, testifying that 'Daniel' was justified in referring to Belshazzar as 'king'. It was they themselves who knew not whereof they wrote.

And so to his credit 'Daniel' scores against his detractor nearly every time:
- Getting the dates right on the Babylonian calendar for the third year of Jehoiakim
- Correctly naming the person, Belshazzar, who was effactually the king when Cyrus captured Babylon
- Nailing the terms that describe the relationship of Belshazzar to Nebuchadnezzar
- Reading the books (*seferim*) correctly to know when *Jeremiah* had predicted the return
- Using the proper ratio of Persian and Greek loan words in the Aramaic passages of his book
- Being theologically ahead of his time on the immortality of the soul
- Being prominent and virtuous enough to be the paragon mentioned in the book of *Ezekiel*

- o Getting appointed to high administrative office, so as to qualify his work for the category of Writings
- o Getting a copy of his book into the Temple in time for Alexander the Great to see it when he visits the Temple in Jerusalem
- o Correctly predicting Alexander's victory over the Persians, to Alexander's delight

We still have no satisfactory answer as to the identity of Darius the Mede. That may appear in time—and since everything else that has shown up has corroborated Daniel's account, we have every reason to expect Darius also to corroborate Daniel. Somehow. We should not let that lacuna deter us.

The modern worldview, from the Renaissance to the twentieth century, rejects miracles *a priori,* full stop, no explanations needed. *Daniel's* fiery furnace, the lions' den, and particularly the miracle of predictive prophecies that actually seem to come true are anathema to the modern world's system of thought. So modernists put *Daniel* as late as they can, to dismiss the book because they think it is a collection of after-the-event 'predictions', dressed up with several miraculous circus acts for comic relief.

But we gathered here are free from such childish constraints. Silverman, the owner of the recently-authenticated Leonardo, tells us that in the art world,

> history is filled with disputes about prove-
> nance and authenticity... We [have]
> long[ed] for surety but often have [had]
> to make do with trust. Now we are enter-
> ing a new era, when science can deliver a
> verdict with a level of proof we are unac-

customed to. A collaboration between connoisseurship and science seems in order.[clxxxii]

In biblical scholarship, too, we must be free to follow the evidence wherever it leads. The art-with-science of archaeology, and the science-with-art of paleography are giving to biblical studies what advanced photography and forensic chemistry give to art, as Professor Zeitlin's work so poignantly demonstrates by his own failure to recognize antiquity when it should be greeted with joy. If this marriage of science with theology leads to a sixth-century Daniel who wrote passages that some say are a spittin' image of Antiochus, who desecrated the Temple temporarily, well, so be it! Even the television pundits get predictions right sometimes. And if the spittin' image turns out to be of the Roman general Titus, who desecrated the Temple by destroying it permanently, well, so much the better![75] As the Psalmist says,

> The kings of the earth take their stand
> And the rulers gather together against the LORD
> And against his Annointed One. . . .
> The One enthroned in heaven laughs;
> The LORD scoffs at them. (Psalm 2:2-4)

An old Jewish saying cuts to the chase: "Man plans, God laughs." Titus' soldiers burned the Temple by mistake, as it were. If Titus' plan had worked, the Jews might have been able to consecrate the Temple yet again in a few months' time, just as they did after Antiochus' folly. But the LORD predicted through Daniel that there would be an abomination of desolation, and a rededi-

---

[75] Titus did not intend to destroy the Temple, but instead to make it a temple to the worship of the Roman Caesar.

cation was not desolate enough to meet that standard. The Temple was apparently destroyed for all time.

Titus' desecration took place long after *Daniel* was well-attested. If God chooses to reveal his sovereignty by slipping his prophets a hot tip now and then, let's not be prudish about it, but recognize it for what it is, and bet accordingly. The LORD sometimes opens the eyes of our faith through his prophets in his Scriptures, even of events to come to pass thousands of years later. Why quibble over a century or two? We now seem to have bounteous evidence pointing to the author 'Daniel' writing in Babylon during the Babylonian exile (605–536).

To summarize: The anti-Jewish and anti-Christian heretic Porphyry was first to suggest that *Daniel* makes after-the-fact prophecies during the period of Antiochus IV Epiphanes, and so must have been written then. But Daniel the man is mentioned in two contexts by 'Ezekiel', implying his presence in Babylon during the exile. Also, Josephus notes that the book of *Daniel* was shown to Alexander the Great in the fourth century BCE. Our Oxfordian friend Pusey points us to several other Second-Temple period authors whose work is dependent on *Daniel*. Multiple copies of *Daniel* dating from the second century BCE have been found at Dead Sea archaeological sites. And Zeitlin gives early rabbinical evidence of *Daniel* first canonized among the Prophets before being elevated to recategorization with the Writings.

Therefore it is much more likely that the book dates from the sixth rather than from the second century

BCE. So this gives Porphyry of Tyre the dubious honor of being first to be colossally wrong about the date *Daniel* was written.

For us in this drawing room, we now have every reason to think that the book of *Daniel* is honest and accurate in its testimony about itself, its historical milieu, its authorship, and its date of composition. This strengthens its hero Daniel's testimony of the Ancient of Days and One like the Son of Man.

Index

Endnotes

[i] This is an endnote. Don't you agree that it is more tedious to find than a footnote?

[ii] Brevard S. Childs, *Introduction to the Old Testament as Scripture* (Philadelphia: Fortress, 1979), 612.

[iii] Bart D. Ehrman, *Forged*, (New York: Harper One, 2011) 115

[iv] Ehrman, Forged,117

[v] Ehrman, Forged, 280

[vi] Jewish Publication Society, *Hebrew-English Tanach*, (Philadelphia: JPS, 2003 – 5764), 1807-08.

[vii] Jewish Publication Society, *Hebrew-English Tanach*, (Philadelphia: JPS, 2003 – 5764), 1821-22.

[viii] Thomas Hoving, *False Impressions: The Hunt for Big-Time Art Fakes* (New York: Simon & Schuster, 1996), 67.

[ix] Frank Spencer, *Piltdown: A Scientific Forgery*, based on research by Ian Langham (1942–1984) (Oxford: Oxford University Press, 1990).

[x] Spencer, *Piltdown*, Back jacket flap.

[xi] Spencer, *Piltdown*, 142.

[xii] Hoving, *False Impressions*, 68.

[xiii] Silverman, *Leonardo's Lost Princess*, 37–38.

[xiv] Thomas Hoving, quoted in Silverman, *Leonardo's Lost Princess*, 36.

[xv] Jerry Pattengale, "How the 'Jesus' Wife' Hoax Fell Apart", *The Wall Street Journal*, May 2, 2014, A11

[xvi] Jonathan Lopez, "A Rembrandt Becomes a Rembrandt Again", *The Wall Street Journal*, May 7, 2014, D5

[xvii] Jonathan Lopez, "A Rembrandt Becomes a Rembrandt Again", *The Wall Street Journal*, May 7, 2014, D5

[xviii] Emanuel Tov, Hebrew Bible, Greek Bible, and Qumran, (Tübingen: Mohr Siebeck, 2008) 303

[xix] E. B. Pusey, *Daniel the Prophet: Nine Lectures Delivered to the Divinity School of the University of Oxford with Copious Notes* (Oxford: James Parker, 1868), 378.

[xx] Pusey, *Daniel*, 380.

[xxi] Milton V. Anastos, "Porphyry's Attack on the Bible", *The Classical Tradition: Literary and Historical Studies in Honor of H. Caplan* (1966), 425–26.

[xxii] *Jerome's Commentary on Daniel*, trans. Gleason L. Archer, Jr. (Grand Rapids: Baker, 1958), 31–32.

[xxiii] Isaac Newton, *Observations Upon the Prophesies of Daniel* (reprint USA: Feather Tail Press, 2009) 16

[xxiv] *Jerome's Commentary*, 31.

xxv Maurice Casey, "Porphyry and the Origin of the Book of Daniel", *Journal of Theological Studies* 82, no. 1 (1976): 16.

xxvi R. K. Harrison, *Introduction to the Old Testament, Vol. 2* (Grand Rapids: Eerdmans, 1969), 1113.

xxvii S. R. Driver, *The Book of Daniel with Introduction and Notes,* The Cambridge Bible for Schools and Colleges (Cambridge: University Press, 1900).

xxviii Childs, *Introduction to the Old Testament,* 612.

xxix Childs, *Introduction to the Old Testament,* 612.

xxx Driver, *The Book of Daniel,* xlvii–xlviii.

xxxi Solomon Zeitlin, *An Historical Study of the Canonization of the Hebrew Scriptures* (Philadelphia: The Jewish Publication Society, 1933), 1.

xxxii Roger T. Beckwith, "The Canon of the Old Testament", in *Understanding Scripture: An Overview of the Bible's Origin, Reliability, and Meaning,* ed. Grudem, Collins, and Schreiner (Wheaton: Crossway, 2012) 74

xxxiii Stephen G. Dempster, "Torah, Torah, Torah: The Emergence of the Tripartite Canon", in *Exploring the Origins of the Bible,* ed. Craig Evans and Emanuel Tov (Grand Rapids: Baker Academic, 2008), 87–128.

xxxiv Zeitlin, *An Historical Study of the Canonization,* 10, note 43.

xxxv Zeitlin, *Canonization,* 18

xxxvi Roger T. Beckwith, "The Canon of the Old Testament", in *Understanding Scripture: An Overview of the Bible's Origin, Reliability, and Meaning,* ed. Grudem, Collins, and Schreiner (Wheaton: Crossway, 2012) 78

xxxvii Zeitlin, *An Historical Study of the Canonization,* 25.

xxxviii Zeitlin, *An Historical Study of the Canonization,* 15.

xxxix Zeitlin, *An Historical Study of the Canonization,* 25.

xl Zeitlin, *An Historical Study of the Canonization,* 25–26.

xli Zeitlin, *An Historical Study of the Canonization,* 18.

xlii Driver, *The Book of Daniel,* xlviii.

xliii Driver, *The Book of Daniel,* xlviiif.

xliv Joyce G. Baldwin, *Daniel: An Introduction and Commentary* (Leicester, England: Inter-Varsity Press, 1978), 20–21.

xlv Baldwin, *Daniel,* 20.

xlvi Driver, *The Book of Daniel,* xlix.

xlvii Baldwin, *Daniel,* 28–29.

xlviii Driver, *The Book of Daniel,* l.

xlix James B. Pritchard, ed., *Ancient Near Eastern Texts Relating to the Old Testament,* 3rd ed. with supplement (Princeton, NJ: Princeton University Press, 1969), 306.

l A. Leo Oppenheim, trans., "Babylonian and Assyrian Historical Texts", in *Ancient Near Eastern Texts,* 3rd ed. with supplement, ed. James B. Pritchard (Princeton: NJ: Princeton University Press, 1969), 309–10, note 5.

li Kenneth A. Kitchen, *The Reliability of the Old Testament* (Grand Rapids: Eerdmans, 2004), 73–74.

lii Driver, *The Book of Daniel,* lii.

liii D. J. Wiseman, "Some Historical Problems in the Book of Daniel", *Notes on Some Problems in the Book of Daniel,* ed. D. J. Wiseman et al. (London: Tyndale Press, 1965), 12.

liv Wiseman, "Some Historical Problems in the Book of Daniel", 13.

lv Allen P. Ross, *Studies in the Book of Daniel*, Beeson Divinity School, Samford University, published on his website, 22.

lvi Wiseman, "Some Historical Problems in the Book of Daniel", 12.

lvii Pritchard, *Ancient Near Eastern Texts* (1969), 306.

lviii Pritchard, *Ancient Near Eastern Texts* (1969), 306.

lix Pritchard, *Ancient Near Eastern Texts* (1969), 306.

lx Pritchard, *Ancient Near Eastern Texts* (1969), 310, note 5.

lxi "Nabonidus Verse Account", in Pritchard, *Ancient Near Eastern Texts* (1969), 313.

lxii H. H. Rowley, *Darius the Mede and the Four World Empires in the Book of Daniel: A Historical Study of Contemporary Theories* (1935; repr., Cardiff: University of Wales Press Board, 1959), 175–76.

lxiii Driver, *The Book of Daniel*, lv.

lxiv Emanuel Tov, *Scribal Practices and Approaches Reflected in the Texts Found in the Judean Desert, Studies on the Texts of the Desert of Judah, vol. 54* (Atlanta: Society of Biblical Literature, 2004), 79.

lxv Driver, *The Book of Daniel*, lv.

lxvi Driver, *The Book of Daniel*, lxiii.

lxvii Driver, *The Book of Daniel*, lvi.

lxviii K. A. Kitchen, "The Aramaic of Daniel", *Notes on Some Problems in the Book of Daniel,* ed. D. J. Wiseman et al. (London: Tyndale Press, 1965), 36–37.

lxix Edwin Yamauchi, *Persia and the Bible* (Grand Rapids: Baker Book House, 1996), 382. cites are Emily Vermeule, *Greece in the Bronze Age* (Chicago: University of Chicago Press, 1972), 71–72; and Emilia Masson, *Recherches*, 19–67.

lxx Driver, *The Book of Daniel*, lviii.

lxxi *The Old Testament Pseudepigrapha,* ed. James H. Charlesworth in two volumes, (Peabody, MA: Hendrickson Publishers, 1983)

lxxii Yamauchi, *Persia and the Bible*, 387.

lxxiii Yamauchi, *Persia and the Bible*, 387.

lxxiv Yamauchi, *Persia and the Bible*, 388.

lxxv Yamauchi, *Persia and the Bible*, 388.

lxxvi Kitchen, *The Reliability of the Old Testament*, 68.

lxxvii *The Old Testament Pseudepigrapha,* ed. James H. Charlesworth in two volumes, (Peabody, MA: Hendrickson Publishers, 1983) 497

lxxviii W. J. Martin, "The Hebrew of Daniel", in *Notes on Some Problems in the Book of Daniel,* ed. D. J. Wiseman et al. (London: Tyndale Press, 1965), 28.

lxxix Martin, "The Hebrew of Daniel", 30.

lxxx Gleason L. Archer, Jr., "The Aramaic of the 'Genesis Apocryphon' Compared with the Aramaic of Daniel", in *New Perspectives on the Old Testament*, ed. J. Burton Payne (Waco, TX: Word Books, 1970), 169. "Comparative Dating for Aramaic of Daniel and the Genesis Apocryphon", delivered before the annual meeting of the Evangelical Theological Society at Westminster Seminary, Philadelphia, December 1968.

lxxxi Driver, *Daniel,* lxiiif.

lxxxii John B. Taylor, *Ezekiel: An Introduction and Commentary,* Tyndale Old Testament Commentaries (Downers Grove, IL: InterVarsity, 1969), 129.

lxxxiii Samuel Sandmel, "Parallelomania", *Journal of Biblical Literature* 81 (1962): 1 – 13

lxxxiv D. A. Carson, *Exegetical Fallacies,* (Grand Rapids: Baker 1984), 43 – 44

lxxxv D. Pardee and Pierre Bordreuil, "Ugarit", in *The Anchor Bible Dictionary,* vol. 6 (New York: Doubleday, 1992), 699.

lxxxvi *The International Standard Bible Encyclopedia,* vol. 4 (Grand Rapids: Eerdmans, 1988), s.v. Ugarit.

lxxxvii Francis I. Andersen, *Job: An Introduction and Commentary,* Tyndale Old Testament Commentaries (Downers Grove, IL: InterVarsity, 1976), 27.

lxxxviii Nicholas Ostler, *Empires of the Word: A Language History of the World* (New York: HarperCollins, 2005), 71.

lxxxix Ostler, *Empires of the Word,* 72.

xc Cyrus H. Gordon and Gary A. Rendsburg, *The Bible and the Ancient Near East,* 4th ed. (New York: W. W. Norton, 1997), 94.

xci Alexander A. Di Lella, "Introduction", *The Book of Daniel,* The Anchor Bible, ed. Louis F. Hartman and Alexander Di Lella (New York: Doubleday, 1978), 8.

xcii Charles F. Pfeiffer, *Ras Shamra and the Bible* (Grand Rapids: Baker, 1962).

xciii Pfeiffer, *Ras Shamra,* 28.

xciv Pfeiffer, *Ras Shamra,* 39.

xcv Pfeiffer, *Ras Shamra,* 63.

xcvi James B. Pritchard, ed., *Ancient Near Eastern Texts* (Princeton, NJ: Princeton University Press, 1955), 150.

xcvii Pritchard, *Ancient Near Eastern Texts,* 151.

xcviii Gordon and Rendsburg, *The Bible and the Ancient Near East,* 91.

[xcix] Simon B. Parker, *The Pre-Biblical Narrative Tradition: Essays on the Ugaritic Poems Karat and Aqhat* (Atlanta: Scholars Press, 1989), 109.

[c] Pusey, *Daniel*, 108.

[ci] Harold H. P. Dressler, "The Ugaritic Dnil and the Daniel of Ezekiel", *Vetus Testamentum* 29, no. 2 (April 1979): 152–61.

[cii] Taylor, *Ezekiel*, 129.

[ciii] Baruch Margalit, "Interpreting the Story of Aqhat", *Vetus Testamentum* 30, fasc. 3, 362; Andersen, *Job*, 62.

[civ] H. H. Ginsberg, "Ugaritic Studies and the Bible", *The Biblical Archaeologist Reader, 2,* ed. David Noel Freedman and Edward F. Campbell, Jr. (Missoula, MT: Scholars Press, 1975), 43.

[cv] Andersen, *Job*, 62.

[cvi] Frederic Raphael, *A Jew among Romans: The Life and Legacy of Flavius Josephus* (New York: Pantheon, 2013), 289.

[cvii] Arnaldo Momigliano, *Alien Wisdom: The Limits of Hellenization* (Cambridge: Cambridge University Press, 1975) 81

[cviii] Marvin H. Pope, *Job*, The Anchor Bible (New York: Doubleday, 1965), xxxvii.

[cix] Pope, *Job*, xxxvi.

[cx] John F. Healey, *Reading the Past,* vol. 9, *The Early Alphabet* (Berkeley: University of California Press, 1990).

[cxi] John Oswalt, *The Bible Among the Myths,*(Grand Rapids: Zondervan, 2009) 172

[cxii] Joseph Rago, "Politics on the Frontiers of Science: The Weekend Interview with Francis Collins", *Wall Street Journal*, November 9, 2013, A13.

[cxiii] George Schlatter, *The Best of Rowan & Martin's Laugh-In Anniversary Special,* a DVD offered as a premium by WQED, Pittsburgh, PA, in 2011.

[cxiv] J. A. T. Robinson, *Redating the New Testament* (London: SCM, 1976), 20.

[cxv] Robinson, *Redating the New Testament*, 20–21.

[cxvi] Luke Timothy Johnson, *The Writings of the New Testament: An Interpretation,* rev. ed. (Minneapolis: Fortress, 1999), 50.

[cxvii] Matt Ridley, "Mind and Matter", *Wall Street Journal,* November 12, 2012, C4.

[cxviii] John J. Collins, *Daniel with an Introduction to Apocalyptic Literature* (Grand Rapids: Eerdmans, 1984), 28.

[cxix] Israel Finkelstein and Neil Asher Silberman, *The Bible Unearthed* (New York: Simon & Schuster, 2001), 298.

[cxx] Finkelstein and Silberman, *Bible Unearthed*, 298.

[cxxi] Finkelstein and Silberman, *Bible Unearthed*, 298.

[cxxii] Thomas Krüger, "Recent Developments in the History of Ancient Israel and their Consequences for a Theology of the Hebrew Bible", a paper presented at the SBL International Meeting in Rome, July 1, 2009, 4.

[cxxiii] William G. Dever, *What Did the Biblical Writers Know and When Did They Know It?* (Grand Rapids: Eerdmans, 2001), 276.

[cxxiv] Paul Landis, *Four Famous Greek Plays* (New York: Modern Library, 1929), xviii.

[cxxv] Pritchard, *Ancient Near Eastern Texts* (1969), 562.

[cxxvi] Pritchard, *Ancient Near Eastern Texts* (1969), 562.

[cxxvii] Emanuel Tov, "Three Strange Books of the LXX: I Kings, Esther, and Daniel Compared with Similar Rewritten Compositions from Qumran and Elsewhere", in *Hebrew Bible, Greek Bible, and Qumran: Texts and Studies in Ancient Judaism* 121 (Tübingen: Mohr Siebeck, 2008), 297.

[cxxviii] Tov, "Three Strange Books of the LXX", note 76.

[cxxix] Solomon Zeitlin, *The Dead Sea Scrolls and Modern Scholarship* (Philadelphia: The Jewish Quarterly Review, 1956), 6.

[cxxx] Zeitlin, *The Dead Sea Scrolls and Modern Scholarship*, 52.

[cxxxi] Zeitlin, *The Dead Sea Scrolls and Modern Scholarship*, 142–47.

[cxxxii] Bonani, Georges et al., "^{14}C Dating of 14 Dead Sea Scrolls", *Radiocarbon* 34, no. 3 (1992): 845.

[cxxxiii] Zeitlin, *An Historical Study of the Canonization,* 25.

[cxxxiv] Solomon Zeitlin, *The Rise and Fall of the Judean State, Vol. I* (Philadelphia: The Jewish Publication Society, 1962), 284.

[cxxxv] Zeitlin, *The Rise and Fall of the Judean State, Vol. I*, 458, note 19.

[cxxxvi] Solomon Zeitlin, *The Rise and Fall of the Judean State, Vol. III* (Philadelphia: The Jewish Publication Society, 1962), 202.

[cxxxvii] Arnaldo Momigliano, *Alien Wisdom: The Limits of Hellenization* (Cambridge: Cambridge University Press, 1975) 82

[cxxxviii] Arnaldo Momigliano, *Alien Wisdom: The Limits of Hellenization* (Cambridge: Cambridge University Press, 1975) 82

[cxxxix] L. Elliott Binns, "The Book of Daniel", in *A New Commentary on Holy Scriptures Including the Apocrypha*, ed. Charles Gore, Henry Leighton Goudge, and Alfred Guillaume (London: SPCK, 1951) 544

[cxl] J. G. Lloyd, *Alexander the Great: Selections from Arrian* (Cambridge: Cambridge University Press, 1981), 35.

[cxli] Aryeh Kasher, "Further Revisited Thoughts on Josephus' Report of Alexander's Campaign to Palestine (Ant 11.304-347)", in *Judah between East and West: The Transition from Persian to Greek Rule (ca. 400–200 BCE)*, ed. Lester Grabbe and Oded Lipschits (London: T & T Clark, 2011), 142–43.

cxlii L. Elliott Binns, "The Book of Daniel", in *A New Commentary on Holy Scriptures Including the Apocrypha*, ed. Charles Gore, Henry Leighton Goudge, and Alfred Guillaume (London: SPCK, 1951) 544

cxliii A. Brian Bosworth, "Plus ca change ...Ancient Historians and Their Sources", *Classical Antiquity* 22, no. 2, 167–98 (Berkeley: University of California Press, 2003), 194.

cxliv Kasher, "Further Revisited Thoughts on Josephus' Report", 142.

cxlv Josephus, *Antiquities of the Jews,* trans. William Whiston (Peabody, MA: Hendrickson, 1987), 307 (11.8.5).

cxlvi Binns, "The Book of Daniel", 545.

cxlvii Tessa Rajak, *Josephus,* 2nd ed. (London: Duckworth, 2002), xi.

cxlviii Lawrence A. Clayton, Vernon James Knight, Jr., and Edward C. Moore, eds., *The De Soto Chronicles: The Expedition of Hernando de Soto to North America in 1539–1543* (Tuscaloosa: University of Alabama Press), 1993.

cxlix Ory Amitay, "The Use and Abuse of the Argumentum ex Silentio—The Case of Alexander in Jerusalem", 3, accessed June 24, 2013, http://amitay.haifa.ac.il/images/7/75/Use_and_abuse_of_argunetum_ex_sil entio.pdf.

cl Amitay, "The Use and Abuse", 7.

cli Amitay, "The Use and Abuse", 7.

clii Josephus, *Antiquities,* 174 (8.6.6).

cliii Pliny the Elder, *Natural History*, vol. 4 (books 12–16), ed. and trans. H. Rackham, Loeb ed. (London: William Heinnemann), 82, n.

cliv Pliny the Elder, *Natural History: A Selection*, trans. John F. Healey, (New York: Penguin Classics, 2004), 6.

clv Pliny the Elder, *Natural History,* vol. 1 (book 1), Loeb ed. (Cambridge, MA: Harvard University), 67.

clvi Amitay cites here Père F.-M. Abel, "Alexandre le Grand en Syrie et en Palestine", *Révue Biblique* 44 (1935): 44–61.

clvii Amitay, "The Use and Abuse", 9.

clviii Josephus, *Antiquities,* 307 (11.8.5).

clix Frank Moore Cross, Jr., "The Papyri and Their Historical Implications", in *Discoveries in the Wadi Ed-Daliheh*, ed. Paul and Nancy Lapp (Cambridge, MA: American Schools of Oriental Research, 1974), 17.

clx Cross, "The Papyri and Their Historical Implications", 18.

clxi Cross, "The Papyri and Their Historical Implications", 20.

clxii Cross, "The Papyri and Their Historical Implications", 19.

clxiii Cross, "The Papyri and Their Historical Implications", 20.

clxiv Cross, "The Papyri and Their Historical Implications", 21.

clxv Roger T. Beckwith, "The Canon of the Old Testament", in *Understanding Scripture: An Overview of the Bible's Origin, Reliability, and Meaning*, ed. Grudem, Collins, and Schreiner (Wheaton: Crossway, 2012) 74 clxvi Kasher, "Further Revisited Thoughts on Josephus' Report", 130–57.

clxvii Kasher, "Further Revisited Thoughts on Josephus' Report", 130.

clxviii Ari Belenkiy, "The Rising of Canopus, the Septuagint, and the Encounter between Shimon the Just and Antiochus the Great", accessed October 14, 2013, www.cs.biu.ac.il/~belenka/Antiochus.pdf.

clxix Binns, "The Book of Daniel", 545.

clxx Pusey, *Daniel,* c (lower case Roman numeral 100).

clxxi Pusey, *Daniel,* 336.

clxxii Pusey, *Daniel,* 356–57.

clxxiii Pusey, *Daniel,* 357.

clxxiv Pusey, *Daniel,* 359.

clxxv Pusey, *Daniel,* 360.

clxxvi Pusey, *Daniel,* 364.

clxxvii Pusey, *Daniel,* 362.

clxxviii C. FitzSimons Allison, *Trust in an Age of Arrogance* (Cambridge, UK: The Lutterworth Press, 2011), 63.

clxxix William Shakespeare, *Hamlet,* Act II.

clxxx Hymn by Thomas Obediah Chisholm, 1866-1960.

clxxxi John Oswalt, *Isaiah* (Grand Rapids: Eerdmans, 1998), 47.

clxxxii Silverman, *Leonardo's Lost Princess*, 50.